simply good food

 *the vegetarian society's*

simply good food

the indispensable guide to vegetarian living

LYN WELLER

Foreword by Tina Fox

HarperCollins*Illustrated*

First published in this edition in 2000 by HarperCollins*Illustrated*, an imprint of HarperCollins*Publishers*.

Previously published by HarperCollins*Publishers* in two separate volumes – *The Vegetarian Society's Health & Vitality Cookbook*, *The Vegetarian Society's Vegetarian Food for Friends*.

Editor: Heather Thomas
Designer: Rolando Ugolini
Photographer: Chris Alack
Indexer: Susan Bosanko

A catalogue record for this book is available from the British Library.

ISBN 0 00 710126 0
Printed & Bound in Italy by Rotolito Lombarda S.p.A.

www.**fire**and**water**.com
Visit the book lover's website

Acknowledgements

Lyn Weller would like to extend her warmest thanks to all the people who have helped in producing this book. In particular, to the staff of the Cordon Vert Cookery School for helping to test the recipes, and the staff from The Vegetarian Society for tasting all the food and coming back for more. Thanks also to Jem Gardener of Vinceremos Wines and Spirits Ltd, Leeds, for providing an interesting selection of vegetarian and vegan wines for many of the recipes, Chris Olivant for his advice and for editing the nutritional information, and The Institute of Brain Chemistry and Human Nutrition for their nutrition software – Foodbase. Finally a very special thanks to my partner, Phil Pugh, for his support throughout the project and for tasting the results, too.

FOREWORD
BY TINA FOX
CHIEF EXECUTIVE, THE VEGETARIAN SOCIETY

The recipes in this latest book from The Vegetarian Society are very wide ranging – from simple and easy-to-prepare, low-fat dishes, to the most indulgent meal you could ever wish to cook for your friends. This is a complete guide to a vegetarian way of living and is ideal for existing vegetarians and vegans or for those just wanting to reduce their meat consumption or start on the path.

Experienced as a tutor and then Manager at the Society's Cordon Vert school, Lyn has a way of making the most interesting food without too much pain and time. We keep her pretty busy so she is very familiar with the time constraints of a busy cook!

The first part of the book focuses on day-to-day cuisine with the added benefit of a low-fat emphasis. The recipes have been garnered from experience over a number of years and have a global flavour in keeping with the new century. The second part concentrates on entertaining – from the easy-going barbecue to more time-consuming but rewarding dinner parties. If you want to make an impression, this is the book for you – a real recipe for success.

Whether you receive this book as a gift or buy it for yourself I am sure you will treasure it for many years to come, and I wish you as much pleasure in using it as I have had testing some of the many recipes.

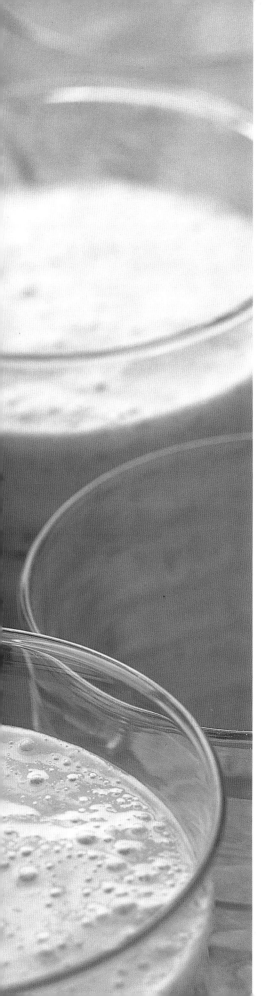

CONTENTS

INTRODUCTION
BY LYN WELLER
CORDON VERT MANAGER, THE VEGETARIAN SOCIETY

Adopting a vegetarian lifestyle that involves a diet which is both healthy and interesting, without leaving you feeling that you're missing out on all the good things in life, is simpler than it may at first appear. *Simply Good Food* gives you colourful, delicious and healthy recipes for both day-to-day eating and for those special occasions when entertaining family and friends. Many of the recipes have a foreign flavour, reflecting the exciting range of international styles taught in the Cordon Vert Cookery School, including imaginative dishes from India, South East Asia, France and the Mediterranean. There are useful hints and tips throughout the book and all the recipes have been tested in the Cordon Vert Cookery School's own kitchens – the home of tasty and imaginative vegetarian cuisine.

Most of the recipes in *Simply Good Food* are quick and easy to prepare, reflecting the constraints of a busy lifestyle, while helping you to avoid relying on processed foods for your daily diet. There are also some more challenging ideas for the times when you want to spend longer in the kitchen trying something new or preparing a more elaborate meal for a special occasion. Also included are menu suggestions to help you experiment with exciting new food combinations. Ideas are given for breakfasts, buffets and parties, picnics and lunches, as well as main courses, dinner parties and a wide selection of delicious (mainly vegan) desserts.

The first section of the book, 'A Healthy Start', concentrates on healthy, everyday eating with chapters covering breakfasts, light meals, main courses, salads, desserts and snacks, sandwiches and drinks. Each recipe has a basic nutritional breakdown and there are suggested menus for different requirements on pages 140-143.

The second section of the book, 'Easy Entertaining', while still being healthy, takes you away from calorie counting into the creative and slightly more indulgent world of entertaining, when food is for sharing with friends and family on a special occasion. Each chapter concentrates on ideas for a different situation: informal suppers, summer and al fresco entertaining, Christmas and winter entertaining, party canapés and finger foods, dinner parties and desserts.

Recipes from both sections of the book can be mixed and matched both within and between each section, depending on your own preferences and creativity. Most recipes are within the capabilities of the average cook and show just how wonderful vegetarian food can be. The majority of the recipes are suitable for a vegan diet or can be adapted, and even those geared towards entertaining tend to be dairy free and consequently fairly low in fat.

The idea behind *Simply Good Food* is the enjoyment of food, and its contents reflect all elements of a vegetarian lifestyle. The planning, cooking and eating of a healthy and vegetarian diet is within everyone's grasp simply by following the recipes and suggestions given. Additionally, creativity, gourmet ingredients, and good wines are an integral part of the book, showing that the finer things in life are central to a vegetarian lifestyle.

Simply Good Food aims to give you an appetite for life by adopting a vegetarian lifestyle. Eat well!

VEGETARIAN NUTRITION

Healthy eating is not about depriving yourself of the things you enjoy, but rather about achieving balance in your diet and educating your palate by making gradual changes towards healthier alternatives. Many people worry that if they stop eating meat and fish and adopt a vegetarian diet they may suffer some nutritional deficiency. However, a vegetarian diet can provide all the nutrients your body needs – from infancy to adulthood – and provided that you maintain a healthy balance there should be no cause for concern. In this introduction to basic vegetarian nutrition, you will discover good vegetarian sources of nutrients and some useful tips to help you achieve a healthy balance in your cooking without losing the flavours and textures that make food so enjoyable.

Research has shown that a vegetarian diet can have a beneficial effect on your health. In general, vegetarians are less prone to suffer from coronary heart disease, hypertension, obesity, various cancers, bowel disorders and diabetes. A vegetarian diet tends to follow the guidelines for healthy eating as laid down by NACNE (National Advisory Committee on Nutrition Education Report 1983), WHO (World Health Organisation 1990) and COMA (Committee on Medical Aspects of Food Policy, three reports COMA 1984, 1991 and 1994), all of which advocate a reduction in fat (particularly saturated fat), an increase in complex carbohydrates and fibre, and a decrease in sugar and salt in the diet. Current healthy eating advice recommends an increase in the consumption of fresh fruit and vegetables together with cereals and pulses. The 'five-a-day' campaign has promoted an increased awareness of the importance of fresh fruit and vegetables in the British diet. If you are a vegetarian, five portions a day should be easy to achieve.

WHAT ARE THE CONSTITUENTS OF A HEALTHY DIET?

There are five classes of nutrient required by our bodies for good health:

- Protein
- Fats
- Carbohydrates
- Vitamins
- Minerals.

We also need fibre and water, which, although having no nutritional content, are necessary for the body to function properly. Most foods contain a range of nutrients but tend to be classified by the predominant one.

PROTEIN

A common question asked by budding vegetarians is 'Will I be able to obtain enough protein without eating meat?' The answer is 'Yes'! Proteins, to build and repair body tissue, are made up from amino acids. There are eight essential amino acids that we must obtain from food because our bodies cannot synthesize them.

Animal protein (meat, dairy products and eggs) contains amino acids in the right proportions, but they are available in plant proteins, too. A single plant source does not usually contain all eight amino acids in the right proportions, but a selection of different plant protein sources will ensure that your body's short-term pool of amino acids, which is drawn on through the day, is kept topped up.

Eating complementary proteins is no longer considered necessary as long as you eat a variety of foods through the day. Combining foods such as pulses and grains, or grains and nuts, will provide a complete protein. The classic examples in a vegetarian diet are beans on toast (pulse and grain), or muesli (grain, nuts and seeds).

If you take a quick look at your diet you should find that within any twenty-four hour period you have almost certainly consumed foods from more than one of these food groups. Vegetarians who consume dairy products (milk, cheese, yogurt, etc.) and eggs can obtain their protein quite easily, but even if you are not following a vegan diet it is unwise to rely on these products as they are also high in saturated fat. When becoming vegetarian, it's easy to fall into the trap of substituting eggs and cheese for meat and in so doing increase rather than decrease your saturated fat intake. Most of the recipes in the first half of this book are or can be dairy free and concentrate on the plant sources of protein which are also low in fat.

FATS

A healthy diet is low in fat, not 'no fat'. Some fat is necessary to keep our tissues in good repair, to manufacture hormones and to act as a carrier for the fat-soluble vitamins A,D,E and K. Fats are made up from fatty acids. Two of these (linoleic and linolenic acid) are termed essential fatty acids (EFAs) as our bodies cannot synthesize them. They occur widely in plant foods. (Vitamin E, a natural antioxidant, is also found in unrefined or cold pressed oils. It protects unsaturated fats and Vitamins A and C in the body as well as cell membranes.) The accepted recommendation is to reduce the amount of fat in our diet overall, and where we do eat fat, the proportion of unsaturated fats (mainly of vegetable origin) should be greater than saturated fats (animal products, coconut and palm oils) or hydrogenated vegetable oils.

CARBOHYDRATES

Carbohydrates provide the 'fuel' or energy for our bodies and enable us to metabolize proteins. They mostly come from plant foods.

- Sugars are simple carbohydrates (monosaccharides) occurring naturally in all vegetable foods, milk and honey. Refined sugars provide sweetness but no nutritional benefit. All sugars play a contributory factor in obesity and dental decay. Unrefined sugars should contain some nutrients, making them preferable when sweetness is required. If you are eating processed foods you are likely to be consuming high amounts of sugar. For example, canned vegetables, baked beans and ready meals usually contain added sugar.

- Complex carbohydrates or starches (polysaccharides) are found in cereals, grains and vegetables. Foods such as bread, pasta, rice, muesli, potatoes and parsnips are good sources of carbohydrates, and a healthy diet should contain plenty of these. Starches provide usable carbohydrate over a long period that keeps the blood sugar level smooth, and as they contain other nutrients their digestion means that vitamins and minerals are gradually released into the bloodstream along with the sugar that provides the energy.

- Dietary fibre (non-starch polysaccharide) is the indigestible part of a carbohydrate food. Fibre helps to expel toxins and waste matter from the body and protects against diseases such as cancer of the colon and diverticular disease.

VITAMINS

Vitamins are chemicals required by the body in small quantities. Mainly the body cannot produce them for itself, so they have to be provided by the food we eat. There are two basic groups of vitamins:

■ water soluble (B group, C and folic acid)
■ fat soluble (A, D, E and K).

The body cannot store water-soluble vitamins so these are needed daily. Vitamins are easily destroyed during storage, processing or cooking. In general, the fresher and less processed the food, the higher the vitamin content. Water-soluble vitamins are destroyed by heat. They are often thrown away in the cooking liquid. Fat-soluble vitamins are more stable but are sensitive to light and air. If you can't obtain really fresh vegetables and use them up quickly, frozen vegetables are often better.

Vitamin A

Plants contain beta-carotene which the body turns into vitamin A, for a healthy skin, the growth of bones, resistance to infection and night vision.

B group

These convert proteins, fats and carbohydrates into energy, for the growth and repair of tissues and skin, for a healthy nervous system and for the production of red blood cells. The vitamin B12 present in plant foods is not readily available to humans and should not be relied on as a safe source. B12 is found in dairy products and fortified foods (e.g. some yeast extracts, soya milks, tofu, cereals and veggie-burger mixes).

Vitamin C

This is required to provide healthy skin, bones, teeth and gums, resistance to infection, wound healing, energy production and growth. It is found in citrus fruits, broccoli, spinach, peppers and berry fruits.

Vitamin D

This is necessary for the production of healthy bones and teeth. Vitamin D is found in dairy products and margarine. It is also produced by the body as a result of the action of sunlight on the skin.

Vitamin E

A natural antioxidant which protects vitamins A and C in the body as well as the cell membranes. Sunflower and other vegetable oils, wheatgerm, hazelnuts and avocados are all good vegetarian sources.

Vitamin K

This vitamin makes blood clot and prevents uncontrolled bleeding. It is found in spinach, cabbage and cauliflower. It is synthesized by the body from bacteria in the intestine. A deficiency is extremely rare.

MINERALS

Seven minerals are found in the body in large quantities. They are calcium, phosphorous, magnesium, sodium, potassium, chlorine and sulphur. All other minerals are required in tiny amounts (less than 100 mg per day) and are called trace minerals.

■ Calcium, phosphorus and magnesium act together. Calcium, for the building and maintenance of strong bones and teeth, is particularly important during childhood, the teenage years and pregnancy. It is found in dairy products, leafy green vegetables, almonds, sesame seeds, dried fruit, pulses and fortified soya milk. Phosphorus and magnesium also help to maintain healthy bones and are used by the body for energy release. Widely found in plant foods, a deficiency is rare. Vitamin D acts with calcium, enhancing its absorption by the body.

■ Sodium, potassium and chlorine are important in maintaining the body's fluid balance (water, blood and other fluids). Most people consume too much sodium which can lead to high blood pressure.

■ Sulphur plays a role in some enzyme systems and a deficiency is rare.

■ Iron is essential for the formation of haemoglobin which transports oxygen in the blood through the body. Iron deficiency is a common nutritional problem in a typical British diet, but vegetarians are no more prone to this than meat eaters. Vitamin C acts with iron to aid its absorption. It is advisable to combine foods that have a high vitamin C content with those containing a high level of iron. E.g. drinking a glass of orange with a meal aids the absorption of iron. The tannin in tea reduces the amount of iron absorbed and shouldn't be drunk an hour on either side of a meal. Leafy green vegetables, pulses, wholemeal bread, dried fruit and pumpkin seeds contain iron.

■ Zinc is necessary for a healthy skin, immune system and resistance to infection as well as helping to heal wounds. Pumpkin seeds are one of the most concentrated sources.

How to plan a healthy diet

Take a look at your current diet and analyse it to see where changes can be made. You can do this, element by element, by following the nutrient list above and asking yourself the following questions:

Proteins

■ Am I too reliant on dairy foods for the protein in my diet?

■ Can I replace some dairy-based meals with one using pulses, grain, nuts and seeds or soya products?

■ Am I taking protein from different plant groups at each meal or at least over the course of a day?

Fats

■ Am I eating too much fat?

■ Just what does 1 teaspoon or 1 tablespoon of oil look like?

■ Am I eating the right balance of fats or am I eating too much saturated fat?

■ Can the saturated fat in my diet be reduced and/or replaced with mono- or poly-unsaturates?

Carbohydrates

■ Am I eating enough starchy foods?

■ Can I reduce the amount of sugar in my diet, not only in drinks but by reducing the amount of processed foods consumed, too?

Vitamins and minerals

■ Am I eating five portions of fruit and vegetables a day? A piece of fruit at breakfast or in place of a sweet dessert can be beneficial.

■ Am I eating a wide range of fresh foods?

General

■ Am I eating a wide variety of food in each category or is my diet in a rut?

Some tips to help you

■ A squeeze of lemon or lime juice or a teaspoon of balsamic vinegar over salad gives a fat-free and simple salad dressing for everyday use.

■ Steam or stir-fry vegetables to minimize nutrient loss.

■ Eat fruit and vegetables raw where possible. A salad every day is a good rule.

■ Keep a food diary for a week or fortnight. Don't worry too much about quantities, but note down all the ingredients. Are you getting 'five-a-day' portions of fruit and vegetables, are you eating too much dairy food, could you reduce the fat, salt and sugar in your diet? Noting it all down for a short period gives you a guide to the constituents of your diet.

■ Use gomasio (10 parts roasted sesame seeds to 1 part salt, ground together), herb salt or a low-sodium 'salt' to reduce your sodium intake.

■ A glass of orange juice (Vitamin C) with a meal helps to increase the absorption of iron.

■ A healthy diet is low in fat but does not exclude fat altogether. The essential fatty acids are obtained from fat, and vitamins A, D, E and K are fat soluble.

■ Complex carbohydrates (starches) are better than sugar for energy. Eat lots of potatoes and pasta.

■ Measure the oil required in a recipe – don't just wave the bottle over the pan – you're bound to overestimate!

■ Cook mushrooms, onion and celery in a little vegetable stock with added shoyu instead of frying them.

■ The greatest vitamin content in fruit and vegetables is just under the skin. Buy organic produce where possible and scrub root vegetables rather than peeling them.

■ Buy your food as fresh as possible and eat it as soon as possible. Stored vegetables lose their vitamin content rapidly and cut vegetables even quicker.

■ Sprout your own beans and seeds in a jar – sprouting beans are highly concentrated in terms of nutrient content.

■ Try to cook your own and freeze an extra portion rather than buying ready meals and processed foods.

■ Beware of replacing meat with cheese. Cheese is high in saturated fat.

■ Chestnuts are low in fat (the only nut that is) so use these in preference to other nuts when possible.

■ Fresh fruit, vegetables and pulses are all good sources of fibre which is an essential part of your diet.

■ Make sure you are getting enough vitamin B12 by spreading your breakfast toast with a teaspoon of fortified yeast extract, or by using a fortified breakfast cereal and soya milk.

■ When buying food, always read the label. Many processed foods unexpectedly contain hidden fats and sugars.

A HEALTHY

START

Health and vitality are the key to a zest for life. All too often 'enjoyment' and 'healthy eating' are thought to be mutually exclusive; however, by ensuring that you eat a balanced vegetarian diet, both can be combined.

This section of the book sets out to give you a variety of colourful and delicious recipes which just happen to be healthy too. Most of the recipes are suitable for everyday eating but one or two main dishes have been written with entertaining in mind. With the busy lives that we all lead today it can be very easy to rely on convenience foods or the same old favourite recipes week in and week out. This section should give you some new ideas and combinations to bring variety to your table.

Each recipe has a nutritional breakdown so that you can see at a glance the amounts of nutrients that you are gaining from each dish, and so choose your own menus based on your particular nutritional requirements. However, the key to healthy eating is variety, so mix and match the recipes and aim to try something new each week to inspire your palate and increase your culinary range, as well as ensuring good nutritional balance. Eat vegetarian, eat healthily and above all eat well!

Healthy
BREAKFASTS

Granola
Home-made soya yogurt with fruit purée
Fruit crêpes
Luxury muesli
Grilled honeyed citrus fruits with yogurt
Baked apple with savoury filling
Baked beans in tomato sauce
Scrambled tofu
Tofu kedgeree
Healthy hash browns with tomatoes and
    rashers
Creamed mushrooms on toast
Field mushrooms stuffed with herby scrambled
    eggs
Herb bread
Seed bread
Cinnamon and raisin bread
Muesli bread
Savoury breakfast rolls
Savoury muffins with sun-dried tomatoes and
    herbs
Breakfast muffins

Left: Savoury breakfast rolls (page 34)
and Breakfast muffins (page 37)

GRANOLA

If you think you don't like muesli, then try this recipe for granola (toasted muesli) as toasting the ingredients brings out their delicious flavours. This unusual breakfast cereal can be stored in an airtight container for a couple of weeks.

225 g/8 oz porridge oats
100 g/4 oz barley flakes
50 g/2 oz wheat flakes
50 g/2 oz sunflower seeds
100 g/4 oz roughly chopped mixed nuts
100 g/4 oz wheat germ
75 g/3 oz desiccated coconut
100 g/4 oz muscovado sugar
150 ml/¼ pint water
150 ml/¼ pint sunflower oil
1 teaspoon vanilla essence
½ teaspoon salt
100 g/4 oz luxury mixed dried fruits
　　(pears, peaches, apricots, etc.), roughly chopped

■ Preheat the oven to 190°C/375°F/Gas Mark 5.
■ Mix the first eight (dry) ingredients together in a bowl. Whisk the water, oil, vanilla essence and salt together in a separate bowl. Add to the dry ingredients and mix well.
■ Spread out on a greased baking sheet and bake in the preheated oven for 30–60 minutes, turning occasionally until evenly browned (to taste).
■ Cool and then stir in the dried fruits. Store in an airtight container. Serve with skimmed, semi-skimmed milk or soya milk.

Serves 16

HOME-MADE SOYA
YOGURT WITH FRUIT PUREE

VEGAN

This recipe is also delicious if eaten unflavoured or with a few drops of vanilla essence added. You can use it as a topping for fruit and desserts (see page 18).

600 ml/1 pint soya milk (unsweetened)
4 tablespoons powdered soya milk* (optional)
1 tablespoon live natural soya yogurt
50 g/2 oz raspberries (or other fruit puréed)
15 g/½ oz icing sugar (optional)

To serve:
whole raspberries
sprigs of mint

■ Bring the soya milk to the boil in a saucepan. Remove from the heat and cool until tepid. Add the powdered soya milk and live yogurt and whisk well to blend.

■ Scald a large vacuum flask with boiling water to sterilize and warm it. Pour in the soya milk mixture. Replace the lid and keep in a warm place, undisturbed, overnight (5–8 hours). Turn out and refrigerate to firm the yogurt**.

■ Press the raspberries through a nylon sieve. Discard the pips. Stir in some icing sugar to sweeten, if liked.

■ Stir the raspberry purée into the yogurt and serve in glass bowls with extra raspberries and a sprig of mint to decorate.

Serves 4

* Available from health food stores. If you are unable to obtain it, you can make the yogurt without, but it will be runnier.

** Save 1 tablespoon of yogurt before adding the fruit, to use as a starter next time. Each time you make it, the yogurt will become thicker and better.

PER SERVING
■
66 kcals (274 kj)
Protein 5 g
Fat 3 g
Carbohydrates 5 g
Fibre 0.3 g

FRUIT CREPES

For this very summery breakfast, you can vary the fruit in the filling according to what is in season. Strawberries with kiwi fruit make a pleasant change, whereas in the winter, orange and grapefruit can be used. Fresh fruit is a good source of Vitamin C.

PER SERVING

316 kcals (1324 kj)
Protein 12 g
Fat 15 g
Carbohydrate 40 g
Fibre 4 g

50 g/2 oz plain white flour
50 g/2 oz gram flour, sifted
15 g/1/2 oz poppy seeds
300 ml/½ pint soya milk
pinch of salt
1 teaspoon sunflower oil
150 ml/5 fl oz natural soya yogurt
  (see page 19)

For the filling:

2 ripe bananas, chopped
juice of 1 lemon
50 g/2 oz ready-to-eat dried
  apricots, chopped
50 g/2 oz toasted almonds, chopped
1 teaspoon groundnut oil

To decorate:

1 teaspoon poppy seeds (optional)
thin slivers of lemon zest

■ To make the pancakes, blend the flours, poppy seeds, soya milk and salt in a blender or food processor. Leave to stand for 20 minutes.

■ Meanwhile, make the filling by mixing the bananas, lemon juice, apricots and almonds together.

■ Heat a little of the oil in a non-stick pancake pan. Use a 50-ml/2-fl oz ladle to measure the batter for each pancake. Pour the batter for one pancake into the pan, swirling it around to cover the base evenly. Cook until set and golden brown underneath, then flip the pancake over and cook the other side. Make 8 pancakes and layer to keep warm.

■ Fill each pancake with a couple of spoonfuls of the filling and fold into quarters. Arrange 2 on each serving plate with a spoonful of soya yogurt. Sprinkle poppy seeds (if using) and lemon zest on the yogurt to decorate and serve.

Serves 4

Opposite: Fruit crepes

LUXURY MUESLI

Many of the ready-made muesli mixes contain not only sugar but also dried milk powder – a product you may wish to avoid if you're following a low-fat, dairy-free or vegan diet.

225 g/8 oz wheat flakes
225 g/8 oz rolled oat flakes (porridge oats)
225 g/8 oz barley flakes
75 g/3 oz each of raw or lightly toasted hazelnuts, almonds, brazil nuts and pecans

75 g/3 oz dates, chopped
75 g/3 oz each of dried figs, apricots, peaches and pears, chopped
175 g/6 oz sultanas
75 g/3 oz raisins
50 g/2 oz dried banana flakes

■ Mix all the muesli ingredients together and store in an airtight container. Serve with milk or soya milk and fresh fruit (e.g. grapes and strawberries).

Makes 30 x 65 g/2½ oz servings

GRILLED HONEYED
CITRUS FRUITS WITH YOGURT

This is a good winter breakfast, high in Vitamin C. By grilling the fruits quickly they are more tempting on a cold day.

1 pink/ruby grapefruit
1 yellow grapefruit
2 large oranges
2 tablespoons liquid honey

pinch of ground cinnamon, cloves and nutmeg
150 ml/5 fl oz low-fat natural yogurt
citrus fruit zest, blanched, to decorate

■ Peel and segment all the citrus fruit and place in a shallow heatproof dish.
■ In a small bowl, mix the honey and ground spices together and then drizzle over the fruit.
■ Preheat the grill to high and place the dish under the grill for 5 minutes, lowering the heat to medium after 1 minute.
■ Serve with natural yogurt, decorated with citrus fruit zest.

Serves 4

BAKED APPLE
WITH SAVOURY FILLING

VEGAN

Baked apples are usually served with sweet fillings, but the tartness of the apple makes a delicious contrast with the savoury ingredients in this recipe – the sort of ingredients that are often used for a vegetarian sausage mixture.

2 teaspoons groundnut oil
1 small onion, very finely chopped
50 g/2 oz mushrooms, very finely chopped
15 g/½ oz walnuts, very finely chopped
15 g/½ oz wholemeal breadcrumbs
2 teaspoons chopped parsley
1 teaspoon chopped sage
salt and freshly ground black pepper
4 Bramley cooking apples

■ Preheat the oven to 190°C/375°F/Gas Mark 5.
■ Heat the oil in a small saucepan and gently cook the onion, mushrooms and walnuts together for about 5 minutes until soft. Remove from the heat and stir in the breadcrumbs, herbs and seasoning to taste.
■ Remove the cores from the apples, then run a sharp knife round the skin in a spiral from top to bottom. Fill the centre of each apple and place on a greased baking sheet.
■ Bake in the preheated oven for 25–30 minutes until the apples are tender when tested with the point of a sharp knife.

Serves 4

PER SERVING
■
128 kcals (541 kj)
Protein 2 g
Fat 3 g
Carbohydrate 25 g
Fibre 4.5 g

BAKED BEANS IN
TOMATO SAUCE

PER SERVING
■
140 kcals (585 kj)
Protein 6 g
Fat 0.6 g
Carbohydrate 30 g
Fibre 5 g

If you are using molasses as a sweetener as in this recipe, try to get unsulphured blackstrap molasses which contain calcium and iron, sometimes in quite significant amounts if iron vats have been used for storage. These baked beans are best made in advance and reheated for breakfast as they take quite a long time to cook.

450 g/1 lb dried haricot beans, soaked overnight in cold water
90 ml/3 fl oz blackstrap molasses
25 g/1 oz dark muscovado sugar
1 teaspoon mustard powder
1 small onion, finely chopped
150 ml/¼ pint passata
2 tablespoons tomato purée
salt and pepper
wholemeal toast, to serve

■ Preheat the oven to 180°C/350°F/Gas Mark 4.
■ Drain the beans and place in a pan of cold water. Bring to the boil. Boil for 10 minutes, then reduce to a simmer and cook until the beans are tender (about 30 minutes). Drain the beans, reserving the liquid, and place in a casserole dish.
■ In a bowl, mix the molasses with 300 ml/½ pint of the reserved liquid. Add the sugar, mustard powder, onion, passata and tomato purée and pour the mixture over the beans.
■ Cover the casserole and cook in the preheated oven for about an hour until the sauce has thickened. Season to taste and serve with wholemeal toast.

Serves 6

SCRAMBLED TOFU

VEGAN

The addition of the fresh vegetables not only adds flavour to this dish but also makes it quite a good source of Vitamin C.

300 g/10 oz firm tofu
1 tablespoon vegetable oil
1 small onion, finely chopped
½ red pepper, deseeded and finely
   diced

1 stick celery, finely diced
50 g/2 oz mushrooms, finely diced
½ teaspoon turmeric
½–1 tablespoon shoyu
freshly ground black pepper

PER SERVING
■
92 kcals (381 kj)
Protein 6 g
Fat 6 g
Carbohydrate 4 g
Fibre 0.8 g

■ Drain the tofu and mash with a fork. Heat the oil in a frying pan and sauté all the vegetables until soft. Add the mashed tofu and turmeric and mix well.
■ Cook for a further 2 minutes, stirring all the time. Season to taste with shoyu and black pepper and serve hot with toast.

Serves 3–4

TOFU KEDGEREE

Kedgeree is often served for breakfast or a light supper. It needs lots of seasoning because the rice absorbs the flavours.

175 g/6 oz long-grain rice
50 g/2 oz butter
225 g/8 oz smoked tofu, drained and
   cut into 1-cm/½-in cubes
pinch of cayenne pepper

2 free-range eggs, hard-boiled
salt and freshly ground black pepper
2 tablespoons tamari
4 tablespoons finely chopped parsley
buttered toast, to serve

PER SERVING
■
270 kcals (1128 kj)
Protein 13.5 g
Fat 18 g
Carbohydrate 15 g
Fibre 0.8 g

■ Cook the rice in slightly salted boiling water until just tender, or according to the packet instructions. Drain and keep warm.
■ Meanwhile, melt the butter in a frying pan and sauté the tofu with a good pinch of cayenne pepper for about 5 minutes, until the tofu starts to colour.
■ Chop the hard-boiled eggs quite finely and add to the pan together with the cooked rice. Heat through thoroughly over a low heat.
■ Season with the salt, pepper and tamari and stir in half of the parsley. Turn into a serving dish and scatter the remaining parsley over the top. Serve with hot buttered toast.

Serves 4

HEALTHY HASH
BROWNS WITH TOMATOES AND RASHERS

Hash browns are usually fried and tend to soak up a lot of oil. This healthier version is baked in the oven and tastes just as good.

450 g/1 lb potatoes, peeled and left whole
1 small onion, grated
1 tablespoon chopped parsley (optional)
1 tablespoon snipped chives (optional)
salt and freshly ground black pepper
1 tablespoon sunflower oil
4 beef tomatoes
1 packet smoked or marinated tofu, cut into 8 thin slices
extra oil, for brushing
sprigs of parsley and snipped chives, to garnish

■ Preheat the oven to 190°C/375°F/Gas Mark 5. Grease 2 baking sheets.
■ Parboil the potatoes in a pan of lightly salted water for about 10 minutes. Drain and leave to cool. Grate coarsely and mix in the onion and herbs (if using), and season well with salt and pepper. Add the sunflower oil and mix to bind.
■ Shape the mixture into 12 patties and place on one of the greased baking sheets. Brush with a little extra oil and bake in the preheated oven for about 20 minutes until golden and tender.
■ At the same time, brush the slices of tofu with a little oil and place on the other greased baking sheet. Cut the tomatoes in half and place on the same baking sheet. Bake in the oven for 25 minutes.
■ Serve immediately, garnished with parsley and snipped chives.

Serves 4

Opposite: Healthy hash browns with tomatoes and rashers

CREAMED
MUSHROOMS ON TOAST

PER SERVING
■
357 kcals (1494 kj)
Protein 11 g
Fat 20.5 g
Carbohydrate 34 g
Fibre 5 g

A delicious breakfast treat at the weekend when you have more time to cook. You can also serve the mushrooms as a good lunchtime snack.

15 g/½ oz butter or vegan margarine*

450 g/1 lb mushrooms, sliced

300 ml/½ pint soured cream or soya cream*

salt and freshly ground black pepper

8 slices wholemeal toast

1 teaspoon paprika

1 tablespoon chopped parsley

■ Melt the butter or vegan margarine* in a saucepan and fry the mushrooms until tender (about 10 minutes). Stir in the cream or soya cream* and season to taste with salt and pepper.

■ Cut the pieces of toast into triangles and arrange on 4 serving plates. Spoon the mushrooms over the top, sprinkle with paprika and parsley and serve.

Serves 4

FIELD MUSHROOMS
STUFFED WITH HERBY SCRAMBLED EGGS

Here's a useful tip for healthy breakfasts when you're serving eggs – if you use a good non-stick pan, you can scramble or 'fry' the eggs without using any fat.

4 very large field mushrooms
4 teaspoons groundnut oil
4 cherry tomatoes, halved
6 large free-range eggs
2 tablespoons finely chopped fresh herbs, e.g. chives, parsley and marjoram
sea salt and freshly ground black pepper

To serve:
6 slices wholemeal toast, cut into triangles
sprigs of parsley and chive flowers

■ Brush both sides of each mushroom with a little oil. Cook gently on both sides under a preheated hot grill until tender and juicy. Grill the cherry tomato halves, cut-side down, until the skin starts to char.
■ Beat the eggs together with the herbs and season to taste with salt and pepper.
■ Heat a heavy-based non-stick pan, and when hot pour in the eggs. Leave them to set for 1 minute, then stir with a wooden spoon, gently but constantly, over a medium heat until the required degree of creaminess is reached. Remove from the heat.
■ Place one mushroom on each warm serving plate. Fill with scrambled eggs. Arrange 3 triangles of toast on each plate, together with 2 grilled cherry tomato halves and a sprig of parsley and some chive flowers. Serve immediately.

Serves 4

PER SERVING
■
239 kcals (1001 kj)
Protein 15 g
Fat 14.5 g
Carbohydrates 14.5 g
Fibre 3 g

HERB BREAD

A delicious bread for weekend guests. Bake it the day before and serve as suggested below.

225 g/8 oz spelt flour
225 g/8 oz strong white flour
good pinch of sea salt
1 teaspoon fennel seed, lightly crushed
1 tablespoon chopped sage
1 tablespoon chopped thyme
15 g/½ oz fresh yeast (or 2 teaspoons dried yeast)
2 teaspoons soft brown sugar
300 ml/½ pint hand-hot water
extra flour, for kneading

PER SERVING
■

390 kcals (1658 kj)
Protein 14.5 g
Fat 2.5 g
Carbohydrate 82.5 g
Fibre 7 g

SERVING SUGGESTION
■

Toast day-old bread, spread with a little mustard if liked, and serve topped with softly scrambled eggs or grilled tomatoes and mushrooms.

■ Preheat the oven to 230°C/450°F/Gas Mark 8. Thoroughly grease a 900-g/2-lb loaf tin or a baking sheet.
■ Sift the flours into a large mixing bowl and add the salt and all the herbs.
■ In a small bowl, cream the fresh yeast with the sugar and add a little of the hand-hot water. Leave in a warm place for about 10 minutes until it starts to froth. (If using dried yeast, add the water first.)
■ Add the yeast to the flour and herb mixture together with enough of the hand-hot water to make a soft but not sticky dough which comes away from the bowl easily.
■ Turn the dough out onto a lightly floured work surface and knead for 10 minutes. Return the dough to a lightly greased bowl, cover loosely with clingfilm and leave to rise until doubled in size (45–60 minutes).
■ Knock the dough back, knead again for 5 minutes, then shape and place in the prepared loaf tin, or shape into a round loaf and place on the baking sheet. Leave to prove for about 20–30 minutes.
■ Bake in the preheated oven for 30–40 minutes. Turn out and cool slightly on a wire cooling rack and serve warm with butter or vegan margarine.

Serves 4

SEED BREAD

PER SERVING

■

113 kcals (477 kj)
Protein 4 g
Fat 3 g
Carbohydrate 19 g
Fibre 2 g

When making bread, try adding the water a tablespoon at a time and mix in well. The dough should be soft, but not sticky, and should come away from the bowl, your hands and the worktop without a trace!

175 g/6 oz strong wholemeal flour
175 g/6 oz strong white flour
good pinch of sea salt
15 g/½ oz fresh yeast (or 2 teaspoons dried yeast)
2 teaspoons sugar
2 teaspoons sunflower oil
300 ml/½ pint (approximately) hand-hot water
1 tablespoon each of sunflower seeds, pumpkin seeds, sesame seeds and
    poppy seeds plus extra for decoration
dairy or soya milk*, to glaze

■ Preheat the oven to 220°C/425°F/Gas Mark 7. Grease a baking sheet.
■ Make the bread, following steps 3–6 of the Cinnamon and Raisin Bread method (see page 32). Then carry on as below.
■ Knock back the dough and add the seeds, kneading them into the dough for about 5 minutes to distribute them evenly.
■ Divide the dough into 6–8 equal pieces and roll each one into a 'sausage' shape, looping one over another to make a knot, and place on the prepared baking sheet. Leave to prove for about 30 minutes.
■ Brush with milk or soya milk* to glaze. Sprinkle some extra seeds on the top, if liked, and bake in the preheated oven for 15–20 minutes. When cooked, the rolls should sound hollow when tapped on the base. Cool on a wire cooling rack.

CINNAMON AND
RAISIN BREAD

Bread doesn't have to be wholemeal to be healthy, and this tasty breakfast bread works best with white flour.

PER SERVING
■
178 kcals (759 kj)
Protein 6 g
Fat 0.7 g
Carbohydrate 40 g
Fibre 2 g

50 g/2 oz raisins
150 ml/¼ pint freshly made tea for soaking
675 g/1½ lb strong white flour
good pinch of salt
15 g/½ oz fresh yeast (or 2 teaspoons dried yeast)
2 teaspoons sugar
1 teaspoon ground cinnamon
grated zest of 1 lemon
450 ml/¾ pint hand-hot water
milk or soya milk*, to glaze

■ Soak the raisins in the tea overnight. Drain and pat dry with kitchen paper.
■ Preheat the oven to 220°C/425°F/Gas Mark 7. Thoroughly grease a 900-g/ 2-lb loaf tin.
■ Sift the flour and salt into a large mixing bowl. In a small mixing bowl, cream the fresh yeast with the sugar and add a little of the warm water. Leave in a warm place for about 10 minutes until it starts to froth. (If using dried yeast, add the water first.)
■ Add the yeast to the flour together with enough water to make a soft but not sticky dough that comes away from the bowl easily.
■ Turn out the dough onto a lightly floured work surface and knead for 10 minutes. Return the dough to a lightly greased bowl, cover loosely with clingfilm and leave to rise until doubled in size (45–60 minutes).
■ Knock the dough back. Mix the raisins, cinnamon and lemon zest in a small bowl, then add to the dough and knead for 5 minutes, incorporating the ingredients as you go. Shape and place in the prepared loaf tin. Leave it to prove for about 20–30 minutes.
■ Brush with milk or soya milk* to glaze and bake in the preheated oven for 35–40 minutes. The bread is cooked when tapping the bottom makes a hollow sound. Turn out onto a cooling rack to go cold before slicing.

Yields 14 slices

MUESLI BREAD

VEGAN

A classic breakfast bread, this is good plain or toasted, with butter or vegan margarine, or a little fruit preserve. It will get you off to a good start for the day.

450 g/1 lb strong wholemeal or spelt flour
good pinch of salt
175 g/6 oz muesli (use ready-made, or see page 22 for Luxury Muesli)
2 tablespoons blackstrap molasses
150 ml/¼ pint warm water
15 g/½ oz fresh yeast (or 2 teaspoons dried yeast)
300 ml/½ pint hand-hot water

■ Preheat the oven to 200°C/400°F/Gas Mark 6. Thoroughly grease two 900-g/2-lb loaf tins.
■ Sift the flour and salt into a large mixing bowl. Then reincorporate any bran left in the sieve. Mix in the muesli and make a well in the centre.
■ In a small bowl, mix the molasses and the warm water together, then mix in the yeast and leave in a warm place for 10 minutes until frothy.
■ Add to the flour mixture with enough of the extra hand-hot water to make a soft but not sticky dough. Turn out onto a lightly floured surface and knead briefly.
■ Divide the dough between the two prepared loaf tins, cover loosely with greased clingfilm and leave in a warm place until doubled in size (about 30 minutes).
■ Remove the clingfilm and bake in the preheated oven for about 40 minutes (until it sounds hollow when tapped). Turn out onto a cooling rack and allow to go cold before slicing.

Yields 14 slices (each loaf)

PER SERVING
■
76 kcals (232 kj)
Protein 3 g
Fat 0.8 g
Carbohydrate 16 g
Fibre 1.5 g

SAVOURY
BREAKFAST ROLLS

This recipe is based on a very old Sussex recipe known as 'Hikers' brunch' or Sussex Sausage Rolls. You can use other fillings to make the rolls really interesting and a surprise to bite into.

175 g/6 oz strong wholemeal flour
175 g/6 oz strong white flour
pinch of salt
good pinch of mixed herbs
15 g/½ oz fresh yeast
1 teaspoon sugar
450 ml/15 fl oz (approx.) hand-hot
    water
1 tablespoon sunflower oil
extra flour, for kneading
450 g/1 lb vegetarian/vegan*
    sausages of your choice (8
    sausages), cooked and cooled

■ Preheat the oven to 220°C/425°F/Gas Mark 7. Grease a baking sheet.
■ Sift the flours and salt into a large bowl. Add the mixed herbs. In a small mixing bowl, cream the fresh yeast with the sugar and add a little of the hand-hot water. Leave in a warm place for about 10 minutes until it starts to froth (if using dried yeast, add the water first).
■ Add the yeast to the flour together with the sunflower oil. Add enough water to make a soft but not sticky dough that comes away from the bowl easily.
■ Turn the dough out onto a floured work surface and knead for 10 minutes. Return the dough to a lightly greased bowl, cover loosely with clingfilm and leave to rise until doubled in size (45–60 minutes).
■ Knock the dough back, knead for a couple of minutes and then cut into 8 equal-sized pieces. Roll each piece out to a rectangle, a little longer than each sausage and about 7.5 cm/3 in wide, and form each piece around a cold sausage – the dough should be about 0.75–1.25 cm/¼–½ in thick all over.
■ Place on the greased baking sheet and leave to rise for about 20–30 minutes until the dough has doubled in size.
■ Bake in the preheated oven for about 15 minutes, then reduce the oven temperature to 180°C/350°F/Gas Mark 4 for a further 20 minutes. Eat warm or cold with the relish of your choice.

Yields 8 rolls

Opposite: Savoury breakfast rolls and Breakfast muffins (page 37)

PER SERVING
■
402 kcals (1698 kj)
Protein 17 g
Fat 9 g
Carbohydrate 68 g
Fibre 6 g

VARIATIONS
■
Try enclosing a tablespoon of garlic mushrooms in each piece of dough, or a tablespoon of Onion Marmalade (see page 107) or even some finely chopped roasted vegetables for a change.

SAVOURY MUFFINS
WITH SUN-DRIED TOMATOES AND HERBS

Muffins are so easy to make and the flavourings can be varied endlessly – use the basic recipe together with your imagination to generate more combinations.

175 g/6 oz plain flour (white or wholemeal)
½ tablespoon baking powder
good pinch of salt
1 large free-range egg, beaten
100 ml/4 fl oz milk
50 g/2 oz butter, softened
25 g/1 oz sun-dried tomatoes (dry – not in oil), finely chopped
good pinch of dried mixed Italian herbs
freshly ground black pepper
25 g/1 oz vegetarian pecorino cheese, very finely grated (optional)

■ Preheat the oven to 200°C/400°F/Gas Mark 6. Line a deep muffin tin with muffin cases.
■ Reconstitute the tomatoes with boiling water, then drain and pat dry with kitchen paper.
■ Sift the flour, baking powder and salt into a large bowl. Add the egg, milk and softened butter, then use a hand whisk to beat all the ingredients together quickly.
■ Quickly fold in the tomatoes and herbs and black pepper and spoon into the muffin cases (each should be about two-thirds full). Sprinkle the top of each one with pecorino, if using.
■ Bake in the preheated oven for about 30 minutes, until well risen and golden in colour. Cool on a wire rack.

Makes 6 large muffins

PER SERVING
■

212 kcals (887 kj)
Protein 6 g
Fat 12 g
Carbohydrate 21 g
Fibre 1 g

SERVING SUGGESTION
■

Serve while still slightly warm with scrambled eggs into which fresh chives have been snipped.

BREAKFAST MUFFINS

Best eaten fresh, these muffins are very quick to make using the all-in-one method.

Basic mixture:
350 g/12 oz plain white flour
1 tablespoon baking powder
175 g/6 oz light muscovado sugar
150 g/50 g butter, softened (or soft margarine)
3 large free-range eggs
150 ml/¼ pint milk

Banana and date:
1 ripe banana, mashed
100 g/4 oz dates, finely chopped

Apple and cinnamon:
1 dessert apple, peeled, cored and grated
½ teaspoon ground cinnamon

■ Preheat the oven to 200°C/400°F/Gas Mark 6. Line a deep muffin tin with muffin cases.

■ Sift the flour and baking powder into a large bowl. Add the sugar and stir well.

■ Add the butter, eggs and milk and whisk together quickly. Put half of the mixture into a clean bowl.

■ Fold the banana and dates into one bowl of the mixture and the apple and cinnamon into the other.

■ Spoon the two mixtures into separate muffin cases (each case should be about two-thirds full).

■ Bake in the preheated oven until well risen and golden (about 15–20 minutes). Cool on a wire rack.

Makes 12 (6 of each flavour)

PER MUFFIN (BANANA AND DATE)
■
245 kcals (1038 kj)
Protein 5.9 g
Fat 2.3 g
Carbohydrate 53.7 g
Fibre 1.8 g

PER MUFFIN (APPLE AND CINNAMON)
■
191 kcals (804 kj)
Protein 5.2 g
Fat 2.3 g
Carbohydrate 40 g
Fibre 1.1 g

APPETISERS
AND LIGHT BITES

Left: Chinese-style lettuce wraps (page 46)

VEGAN

TUSCAN
TOMATO SOUP

PER SERVING

■

230 kcals (965 kj)
Protein 7 g
Fat 8 g
Carbohydrate 35 g
Fibre 3 g

This very simple rustic soup would be made in Italy with fresh tomatoes, but to improve the flavour a mixture of passata and roasted tomatoes is used here. The bread gives an unusual texture to the soup, which you can serve for a substantial lunch.

450 g/1 lb ripe, full-flavour tomatoes
4 garlic cloves, skins left on
2 tablespoons olive oil
1 onion, finely chopped
450 g/1 lb passata
1 litre/1¾ pints tomato and herb stock
   (made with stock cubes)
1 small baguette
1 small bunch of basil
salt and freshly ground black pepper

■ Preheat the oven to 200°C/400°F/Gas Mark 6.
■ Place the tomatoes and garlic in a roasting pan and drizzle with 1 tablespoon olive oil. Roast in the preheated oven for about 1 hour until the skins are blackening. Remove the garlic after 30 minutes and skin.
■ Heat the remaining oil in a large saucepan and fry the onion until soft and golden. Add the roasted tomatoes with all their juices, the garlic, passata and stock. Bring to the boil, then cover the pan and simmer for 30 minutes.
■ Remove from the heat and cool before blending the soup thoroughly in a blender or food processor, making sure that all the tomato skins are blended. Return the soup to a clean saucepan.
■ Cut the ends off the baguette and discard. Cut the baguette into small cubes and stir into the soup while reheating. Cook gently for about 10 minutes.
■ Tear the basil leaves into rough pieces and add to the soup just before serving. Season to taste with salt and pepper and serve in a tureen or individual bowls.

Serves 4

WATERCRESS SOUP

Watercress is full of iron and vitamin C. This soup freezes well and keeps for about two to three months, and can be reheated from frozen.

PER SERVING
■
122 kcals (509 kj)
Protein 4.5 g
Fat 5 g
Carbohydrate 9 g
Fibre 1 g

2 teaspoons sunflower oil
1 onion, finely chopped
100 g/4 oz potatoes, peeled, diced, rinsed and drained
2 bunches of watercress
900 ml/1½ pints vegetable stock
juice of 1 orange
150 ml/¼ pint soya milk
1 tablespoon shoyu or tamari
pinch of ground nutmeg
salt and freshly ground black pepper
4 teaspoons soya cream
sprigs of watercress and orange zest, to garnish

■ Heat the oil in a large saucepan. Sauté the onion and potatoes for 5 minutes.

■ Chop the watercress leaves and stalks, discarding any really woody pieces. Add to the pan with the stock and orange juice. Bring to the boil, then cover the pan and simmer gently for 15–20 minutes.

■ Remove from the heat and cool, then blend in a blender or food processor until smooth.

■ Return to the heat and add the soya milk and shoyu or tamari. Reheat gently and season to taste with nutmeg, salt and pepper.

■ Serve the soup immediately in individual bowls, topped with a swirl of soya cream and garnished with watercress sprigs and orange zest.

Serves 4

VEGAN

CARROT SOUP

Carrots, like many other orange and red vegetables, are high in betacarotene which the body converts to Vitamin A.

PER SERVING
■
93 kcals (386 kj)
Protein 2 g
Fat 3 g
Carbohydrate 16 g
Fibre 5 g

1 onion, chopped	salt and freshly ground black pepper
1 garlic clove, chopped	900 ml/1½ pints light vegetable stock
1 tablespoon oil	1 tablespoon chopped parsley or
675 g/1½ lb carrots, chopped	fresh coriander, to garnish
1 teaspoon grated fresh ginger root	

■ Sauté the onion and garlic in the oil for 5 minutes in a covered pan without browning. Add the carrots, ginger and a sprinkling of salt. Cover and lightly fry for a further 10 minutes, stirring occasionally.

■ Add the stock, bring to the boil, then reduce the heat and simmer for 15 minutes, or until the carrots are tender. Purée the soup in a blender, then return to the pan and reheat. Serve garnished with chopped fresh herbs.

Serves 4

MISO SOUP

VEGAN

Miso is a savoury paste made from fermented soya beans and is used to flavour soups, stews, pâtés, etc. Use sparingly.

PER SERVING
■
95 kcals (399 kj)
Protein 5 g
Fat 3 g
Carbohydrate 12 g
Fibre 1 g

1 teaspoon groundnut oil	100 g/4 oz mooli (daikon/white
2 onions, thinly sliced	radish)
2 garlic cloves, crushed	15 g/½ oz aramé, soaked for 10
2.5-cm/1-in piece fresh root ginger,	minutes
peeled and grated	3 tablespoons barley miso
900 ml/1½ pints vegetable stock	2 spring onions, shredded, to garnish

■ Heat the oil and sauté the onions and garlic for about 5 minutes. Add the ginger, vegetable stock, mooli and aramé. Bring to the boil, then reduce the heat and simmer gently for 15–20 minutes.

■ Put the miso into a small bowl and cream it with a little of the hot soup. Pour into the saucepan and stir well. Serve garnished with spring onions.

Serves 4

Opposite: Carrot soup and Miso soup

VEGAN

PUMPKIN
AND HARICOT BEAN SOUP

Pumpkins are harvested in the autumn and are often hollowed out and carved into a wicked face lantern for Hallowe'en. However, pumpkin is delicious to eat and there are many different varieties to choose from. Pumpkin has a high water content so you may lose some of the bulk when you cook it. This nutritious soup is excellent for serving at a Hallowe'en party as you can use the flesh for making the soup, then carve the shell into a lantern. If you can't buy a pumpkin, use butternut squash instead.

PER SERVING
■
227 kcals (948 kj)
Protein: 8 g
Fat: 4.5 g
Carbohydrate: 41 g
Fibre: 9 g

1 tablespoon olive oil
1 large onion, finely chopped
2 garlic cloves, crushed
675 g/1½ lb pumpkin flesh, cubed
450 g/1 lb sweet potatoes, peeled and cubed
1 teaspoon mixed dried herbs
1 teaspoon chopped sage
1.5 litres/2½ pints vegetable stock
400-g/14-oz can of haricot beans, rinsed and drained
salt and freshly ground black pepper

■ Heat the oil in a large saucepan and gently fry the onion and garlic for about 10 minutes until softened and starting to colour. Add the pumpkin, sweet potato and herbs and cook gently for 5 minutes.
■ Add the vegetable stock and bring to the boil. Cover the pan and simmer for 30 minutes until the vegetables are cooked and tender.
■ Add the haricot beans and season to taste with salt and pepper. Cook for 5 minutes, then serve hot with crusty bread.

Serves 4

CHICK PEA
AND SPINACH SOUP

VEGAN

Chick peas are high in protein and phosphorus, sulphur and potassium. They are one of the most popular and tasty pulses and can even be sprouted to increase their nutritional value.

2 teaspoons sunflower oil
1 onion, finely chopped
1 garlic clove, crushed
1 teaspoon cumin seeds, lightly crushed
100 g/4 oz potato, diced and rinsed under running cold water
900 ml/1½ pints vegetable stock
400 g/14 oz can chick peas, rinsed, drained and roughly chopped
100 g/4 oz finely chopped spinach
2 tablespoons shoyu
salt and freshly ground black pepper

■ Heat the oil in a large saucepan. Sauté the onion, garlic and cumin seeds together for 5 minutes until starting to soften.

■ Drain the potatoes and add to the onions. Continue to cook for 5 minutes, stirring occasionally. Add the stock and bring to the boil. Cover the pan, reduce the heat and simmer for 15–20 minutes until the potatoes are cooked. Add the spinach and cook for 2 minutes.

■ Remove from the heat, add half of the chick peas and blend the soup in a food processor, using the pulse button to thicken the soup, until smooth.

■ Return to the pan, add the remaining chick peas, shoyu and seasoning to taste. Reheat thoroughly for 5–10 minutes and serve immediately with fresh crusty bread.

Serves 4

PER SERVING
■

177 kcals (745 kj)
Protein 10 g
Fat 5.5 g
Carbohydrate 24 g
Fibre 5 g

CHINESE-STYLE
LETTUCE WRAPS

PER SERVING

■

113 kcals (471 kj)
Protein 4 g
Fat 5 g
Carbohydrate 12 g
Added sugar 5 g
Fibre 0.5 g

An interesting dish to serve as a starter for an oriental meal, these wraps will be a talking point. Tofu is an excellent vegetarian source of protein.

100 g/4 oz firm tofu
2 tablespoons shoyu
1 garlic clove, crushed
2.5-cm/1-in piece fresh root ginger, peeled and grated
1 tablespoon liquid honey
15 g/½ oz dried shiitake mushrooms
1 tablespoon groundnut oil
1 small onion, very finely chopped
50 g/2 oz water chestnuts, finely shredded
50 g/2 oz bamboo shoots, finely shredded

salt, to taste
1 teaspoon sesame oil
8 large iceberg lettuce leaves

For the dipping sauce:
50 ml/2 fl oz shoyu
1 tablespoon mirin (or vegetarian sherry)
2.5-cm/1-in piece fresh root ginger, peeled, grated and squeezed
few drops of tabasco sauce
1 teaspoon sesame oil

■ Finely chop the tofu (to resemble mince). Mix the shoyu, garlic, ginger, and honey together and marinate the tofu in this mixture for 30 minutes or longer.

■ Cover the dried shiitake mushrooms with boiling water and leave to soak for 20 minutes. Drain, discard the stalks and chop the mushrooms finely.

■ For the dipping sauce, mix all the ingredients together and place in a small bowl.

■ Heat the groundnut oil in a frying pan and fry the onion for 2 minutes. Add the marinated tofu together with any remaining marinade, the mushrooms, water chestnuts, bamboo shoots and salt to taste. Fry gently for about 3 minutes. Stir in the sesame oil.

■ Place 1–2 tablespoons of the mixture in the centre of each lettuce leaf. Fold in the sides and roll into a neat parcel (secure with a cocktail stick if necessary). Serve immediately with the dipping sauce.

Serves 4

Opposite: Chinese-style lettuce wraps

BROAD BEAN,
LEMON AND SAGE DIP

PER SERVING
■

97 kcals (403 kj)
Protein 7 g
Fat 6 g
Carbohydrate 4 g
Fibre 2 g

Broad beans are in season from the end of May through to the end of July, but as the season progresses they tend to become tougher. If you are using fresh broad beans, you need 100 g/4 oz of shelled beans for this recipe. Frozen broad beans are also good and almost as nutritious as freshly picked beans. The combination of flavours in this dip has a really fresh taste. Make it a little thicker and use it as a sandwich filling with crisp lettuce leaves or rocket.

1 tablespoon sunflower oil
1 small onion, finely chopped
225 g/8 oz silken tofu
1 garlic clove, crushed
zest and juice of 1 lemon
5 tablespoons soya milk
1 tablespoon shoyu
1 tablespoon chopped sage leaves
100 g/4 oz broad beans, cooked
salt and freshly ground black pepper

■ Heat the oil and gently fry the onion until softened. Cool.
■ Drain the silken tofu and place in a blender. Add the crushed garlic, lemon juice and half of the lemon zest together with the soya milk, shoyu, sage and broad beans. Blend to a smooth dipping consistency.
■ Season to taste and serve in a bowl, garnished with the reserved lemon zest, with raw vegetable crudités and pitta bread fingers.

Serves 4

MINTY PEA DIP

VEGAN

Frozen peas are a good source of vitamin C. This dip is a vivid bright green in colour, so there is no mistaking the main ingredient!

225 g/8 oz frozen peas
15 g/½ oz chives, snipped
15 g/½ oz mint leaves, chopped
½ green chilli, deseeded and finely
  chopped

grated zest and juice of ½ lemon
pinch of salt
extra lemon zest and mint leaves, to
  garnish
vegetable crudités, to serve

PER SERVING
■
40 kcals (171 kj)
Protein 4 g
Fat 0.6 g
Carbohydrate 6 g
Fibre 3 g

- Place the peas in a sieve and pour boiling water over to thaw them.
- Blend all the ingredients to a smooth purée. (If necessary, add a little water to thin the mixture.) Season to taste and transfer to a serving dish.
- Cover and set aside at room temperature for 30 minutes before serving, to allow the flavours to develop. Serve, garnished with lemon zest and herbs, with a selection of vegetable crudités.

Serves 4

ITALIAN PATE

*CAN BE VEGAN

Ricotta and cottage cheese are both low in fat and add flavour and texture. For a dairy-free version use silken tofu*.

225 g/8 oz ricotta (or cottage
  cheese or silken tofu*)
I tablespoon fine   chopped
2 ripe tomatoes, skinned, deseeded
  and finely chopped

1–2 tablespoons finely chopped basil
I teaspoon vegan horseradish sauce
  (or   rd)
few sprigs of basil, to garnish

PER SERVING
■
70 kcals (298 kj)
Protein 8 g
Fat 2 g
  hydrate 6 g

- Drain the ricotta (or cottage cheese or silken tofu*, if using) and push through a sieve. In a large bowl, mix together all the ingredients, stirring gently. Cover the bowl with clingfilm and chill slightly before serving.
- Serve the pâté in a small bowl, or place individual servings on each plate garnished with fresh herbs.

Serves 4

FATTOUSH WITH LAMB'S LETTUCE

This substantial salad is suitable for serving as a light meal. If you want to avoid using the cheese and egg, try substituting finely chopped, grilled smoked or marinated tofu.

PER SERVING
■

141 kcals (589 kj)
Protein 7 g
Fat 10 g
Carbohydrate 7 g
Fibre 2 g

½ cos lettuce, washed and shredded
50 g/2 oz lamb's lettuce, washed
4 ripe tomatoes, each cut into
   8 wedges
¼ cucumber, diced
5 spring onions, finely sliced
12 kalamata olives, stoned
15 g/½ oz mint, chopped
15 g/½ oz parsley, chopped
75 g/3 oz feta cheese, diced (omit
   for vegan*)
2 free-range eggs, hard-boiled (omit
   for vegan*)

For the dressing:
juice of 1 lemon
2 tablespoons olive oil
1 teaspoon wholegrain mustard
1 teaspoon chopped mint
1 teaspoon chopped parsley
1 garlic clove, crushed
salt and freshly ground black pepper

For the croûtons:
2 slices white bread, toasted and
   crusts removed
1 garlic clove, peeled

■ Make the dressing by whisking all the ingredients together until thoroughly blended.

■ Mix the lettuces, tomatoes, cucumber, spring onions, olives, mint and parsley together in a bowl. Pour over the dressing and toss well. Turn into a salad bowl.

■ If using the feta cheese, scatter over the salad and mix in. If using the hard-boiled eggs, shell and chop finely and sprinkle over the salad.

■ Rub the whole garlic clove over the surface of each piece of toast. Cut the toast into bite-sized croûtons and scatter over the salad. Serve immediately.

Serves

Opposite: Fattoush with lamb's lettuce

Malaysian
VERMICELLI

Marinated tofu pieces are extremely useful for stir-fries or stews. You can buy packs of these tofu chunks in health food stores or supermarkets. They have been partly cooked so that they keep their shape and texture well when added to a dish.

PER SERVING
■
213 kcals (889 kj)
Protein 11 g
Fat 8.5 g
Carbohydrate 27 g
Fibre 2 g

2.5-cm/1-in piece of cinnamon
  stick
4 green cardamoms
1 teaspoon coriander seeds
1 teaspoon cumin seeds
6 whole cloves
1 tablespoon groundnut oil
1 large onion, finely chopped
2 garlic cloves, crushed
½ teaspoon chilli powder
400-g/14-oz can of chopped
  tomatoes, drained

2.5-cm/1-in piece fresh root ginger,
  peeled, grated and juice squeezed
  out
juice of 1 lemon
225 g/8 oz marinated tofu pieces,
  roughly chopped
150 ml/¼ pint water
salt, to taste
200 g/7 oz beansprouts
75 g/3 oz rice vermicelli, cooked
25 g/1 oz roasted peanuts, chopped

■ Heat a dry non-stick frying pan and add all the whole spices. Toss in the pan until they release their aromas, and then grind to a fine powder.

■ Heat the groundnut oil in a wok and cook the onion and garlic for about 5 minutes until lightly browned. Add the ground spices and chilli powder and cook for 2 minutes. Add the tomatoes and cook for 5 more minutes to a chunky paste.

■ Add the ginger, lemon juice, tofu and water and bring to the boil, stirring. Reduce the heat and simmer gently for about 5–10 minutes until the sauce thickens.

■ Season to taste with salt and pepper, add the beansprouts and cook for 2 minutes. Add the vermicelli and toss well to coat in the tofu sauce. Scatter the chopped roasted peanuts over the top and serve immediately.

Serves 4

BURMESE-STYLE
STIR-FRY

There are lots of fresh vegetables in this dish and as they are cooked quickly by stir-frying, the vitamin content remains high. Although the fat content is quite high, you drain the fried tofu on kitchen paper to remove any excess.

250 g/9 oz firm regular tofu
4 tablespoons groundnut oil

Stir-fry:
375 g/12 oz egg-free noodles
1 teaspoon groundnut oil
2 shallots, sliced
4 garlic cloves, finely chopped
1 red chilli, finely chopped
50 g/2 oz bamboo shoots, shredded
50 g/2 oz water chestnuts, sliced
50 g/2 oz baby sweetcorn, halved lengthways
100 g/4 oz Chinese leaves, shredded
100 g/4 oz baby spinach leaves, shredded
100 g/4 oz beansprouts
2 tablespoons shoyu
1 teaspoon sesame oil

PER SERVING
■
260 kcals (1081 kj)
Protein 10 g
Fat 16 g
Carbohydrate 19 g
Fibre 2 g

■ Drain and press the tofu to remove excess liquid. Cut into cubes and then into triangles. Heat the oil in a non-stick frying pan and fry the tofu until golden on both sides. Drain well on kitchen paper and keep warm.

■ Cook the noodles, according to the packet instructions, for about 4 minutes. Drain and keep warm.

■ In a wok, heat the groundnut oil. When very hot, add the shallots, garlic and chilli and cook, stirring all the time, until golden. Add the bamboo shoots, water chestnuts and sweetcorn and cook for 2 minutes.

■ Add the shredded Chinese leaves and spinach and stir-fry for 2–3 minutes until the spinach has wilted. Add the beansprouts and reserved tofu and mix well. Stir in the shoyu and sesame oil and serve on a bed of noodles.

Serves 4

POTATO PIZZA WITH
MIXED PEPPER AND MUSHROOM TOPPING

PER SERVING

■

259 kcals (1089 kj)
Protein 7 g
Fat 9 g
Carbohydrate 39 g
Fibre 5 g

The potatoes make a much lighter base than a traditional bread pizza, and the colourful pepper and mushroom topping is a good source of vitamins.

225 g/8 oz potatoes, chopped
25 g/1 oz butter or vegan margarine*
salt and pepper
100 g/4 oz self-raising flour (white)
2 tablespoons tomato purée
1 tablespoon olive oil
1 large onion, sliced
1 red pepper, deseeded and sliced
1 orange or yellow pepper, deseeded and sliced
1 green pepper, deseeded and sliced
100 g/4 oz mushrooms, sliced
1 teaspoon dried oregano
1 tablespoon cider vinegar
225 g/8 oz spinach leaves
2 tablespoons vegetarian Parmesan cheese (optional)

■ Preheat the oven to 200°C/400°F/Gas Mark 6.
■ Boil the potatoes in a large pan of salted water until tender. Drain well and mash with the butter or margarine* until smooth. Season with salt and pepper.
■ While still warm, stir in the flour, and then turn out onto a lightly floured worktop and knead for 2 minutes. Press into a round on a greased baking sheet, using your fingers, and spread the tomato purée evenly over the surface.
■ Heat the olive oil in a frying pan. Fry the onion and peppers for 5 minutes until starting to soften, then add the mushrooms and cook for a further 5 minutes until tender. Stir in the dried oregano, cider vinegar and seasoning. Remove from the heat.
■ Wash the spinach leaves thoroughly and cook gently in a covered pan for 2 minutes in the water remaining on the leaves until bright green and wilted. Drain well.
■ Spread the spinach leaves evenly over the pizza base, followed by the onion mixture. Sprinkle with Parmesan, if using, and bake in the preheated oven for 20–30 minutes until the edges of the base look golden and crispy. Serve immediately with a green salad.

Serves 4

Opposite: Potato pizza with mixed pepper and mushroom topping

ROAST PEPPER
AND AUBERGINE MOUSSE

High in beta-carotene, the red peppers also give this mousse a distinctive colour. This dish makes a delicious light lunch or a good dinner party starter.

1 aubergine	1 garlic clove, crushed
1 teaspoon groundnut oil	salt and freshly ground black pepper
2 large red peppers	2½ tablespoons agar agar flakes
juice of 1 lemon	125 ml/5 fl oz water
225 g/8 oz silken tofu	sprigs of parsley, to garnish
150 ml/¼ pint soya milk	melba toasts, to serve

■ Preheat the oven to 180°C/350°F/ Gas Mark 4.

■ Brush the aubergine with the oil, place on a baking sheet with the red peppers and bake in the preheated oven for 45 minutes.

■ Allow to cool a little, then peel the aubergine, and skin and deseed the peppers, reserving the juices. Chop the flesh, reserving a few strips of red pepper for the garnish.

■ Put the flesh and reserved juices in a blender or food processor with the lemon juice, tofu, soya milk, crushed garlic and seasoning. Blend until smooth.

■ Put the agar agar and water in a saucepan. Heat gently at first, then bring to the boil, stirring all the time. Simmer for 5–10 minutes until completely dissolved.

■ Stir the agar agar into the pepper and aubergine mixture and blend again. Pour immediately into individual ramekin dishes, tapping each one sharply on the worktop to remove any air bubbles. Refrigerate for at least 30 minutes to set.

■ Decorate with the reserved red pepper strips and serve garnished with parsley sprigs with the melba toasts.

Serves 6

CAPONATA CROSTINI

VEGAN

Traditional crostini bases are brushed with oil before baking in the oven, but you can make a low-fat version quite simply by omiting the oil and baking the bread dry – it won't be as golden, but it will still be crisp.

1 baguette, cut into 1.25-cm/½-in thick slices
2 large garlic cloves, left whole
3 plum tomatoes, skinned and roughly chopped
1 small red onion, finely sliced
100 g/4 oz stoned green olives, roughly chopped
1½ tablespoons capers
25 g/1 oz pine kernels
salt and freshly ground pepper
flat-leaf parsley, to garnish

- Preheat the oven to 200°C/400°F/Gas Mark 6.
- Place the bread slices on a baking sheet and bake in the preheated oven until golden – rub with the whole cloves of garlic.
- Mix the tomatoes, onion, olives, capers and pine kernels together and season well. Pile the mixture on top of the crostini bases and garnish with flat-leaf parsley.

Serves 6

PER SERVING
■
282 kcals (1194 kj)
Protein 9 g
Fat 7 g
Carbohydrate 48 g
Fibre 2 g

ROAST VEGETABLE
TORTILLAS WITH FROMAGE FRAIS AND MINT DRESSING

Fromage frais contains between one and eight per cent fat, so it is ideal for low-fat dressings. Check the label to make sure that it is suitable for vegetarians as it may be thickened with animal rennet.

PER SERVING
■

407 kcals (1711 kj)
Protein 15 g
Fat 12 g
Carbohydrate 64 g
Fibre 7 g

2 tablespoons olive oil
salt and freshly ground black pepper
1 garlic clove, crushed
1 aubergine, cubed
3 courgettes, cubed
1 red pepper, deseeded and cubed
1 yellow pepper, deseeded and
　　cubed
8 shallots, halved
12 garlic cloves, peeled and left
　　whole
1 bulb fennel, diced
100 g/4 oz cherry tomatoes, halved

25 g/1 oz pine nuts, toasted
few drops of Tabasco
8 large soft flour tortillas
sprigs of mint, to garnish

**Fromage frais
and mint dressing:**
200 g/7 oz very low fat natural
　　fromage frais
15 g/½ oz fresh mint
2 teaspoons white wine vinegar
1 teaspoon apple juice concentrate

■ Preheat the oven to 200°C/400°F/Gas Mark 6.
■ Mix the olive oil, salt and pepper and crushed garlic together.
■ Put all the vegetables, except the cherry tomatoes, in a roasting pan. Pour over the olive oil mixture and toss well to coat. Roast in the preheated oven for 25 minutes.
■ Stir the vegetables around and add the cherry tomatoes and roast for a further 5–10 minutes until the vegetables are cooked and starting to char a little.
■ Remove from the oven and stir in the pine nuts and a few drops of tabasco. At the same time, wrap the tortillas in foil and warm through in the oven for 10 minutes.
■ Meanwhile, make the dressing by beating all the ingredients together.
■ Divide the roast vegetable mixture equally between the warm tortillas. Roll up and serve immediately with the dressing drizzled over them, garnished with sprigs of mint.

Serves 4

SAVOURY FILO
TRIANGLES

These filo triangles are delicious made with tofu, but if you prefer dairy foods, substitute ricotta or cottage cheese.

225 g/8 oz filo pastry
2 tablespoons olive oil

Tofu and spinach filling:
1 small onion, finely chopped
1 tablespoon olive oil
50 g/2 oz crumbled tofu*/ricotta cheese
1 tablespoon tahini
25 g/1 oz stoned olives, chopped
150 g/5 oz spinach, blanched, drained and chopped (if frozen, thawed, drained and chopped)
25 g/1 oz breadcrumbs
pinch of freshly grated nutmeg
15 g/½ oz basil leaves, chopped
salt and pepper

■ Preheat the oven to 190°C/375°F/Gas Mark 5.
■ To make the filling, sauté the onion gently in the oil until soft and golden.
■ In a bowl, cream the tofu* or ricotta with the tahini until smooth. Mix in all the remaining ingredients, including the onion, and season to taste with salt and pepper.
■ Cut the filo sheets into 8-cm/3-in × 30-cm/12-in strips. Use 2 strips at a time, keeping the rest covered. Brush one strip lightly with olive oil, then place the second strip on top and brush lightly again.
■ Place 1 tablespoon of the filling mixture on one end of the strip. Fold the corner of the pastry over the filling to make a triangle and continue folding up the length of the strip, maintaining a triangular shape as you go. Repeat the filling and folding process with all the filo strips.
■ Place on an oiled baking sheet (with sides) and bake in the preheated oven for about 20 minutes until crisp and golden.

Serves 6

PER SERVING
■
191 kcals (795 kj)
Protein 5 g
Fat 8.5 g
Carbohydrate 25 g
Added sugar 0.9 g
Fibre 1 g

MAIN-COURSE
DISHES

Bubble and squeak patties
Farfalle with mange tout, flageolet beans, courgettes and mint
Penne with broccoli, avocado and roast pepper
Asparagus fettucine stir-fry with peanut sauce
Millet pilaf
Wild mushroom risotto
Vegetable and black eye bean bangalore
Mushroom, pepper and tomato stew with quinoa
Nutty flan with tofu and vegetable filling
Sweet and sour cabbage parcels
Enchiladas with warm tomato salsa
Szechuan tofu
Marinated tofu and vegetable filo pie
Broad bean and sweetcorn stew
Patatas bravas
Spiced red cabbage
Quick-fried shredded kohlrabi
Sweet baked beetroot
Celeriac mash
Teriyaki stir-fry

Left: Nutty flan with tofu and vegetable filling (page 72)

*CAN BE VEGAN

BUBBLE AND SQUEAK
PATTIES

PER SERVING
■

228 kcals (956 kj)
Protein 7 g
Fat 10 g
Carbohydrate 28 g
Fibre 4 g

This combination makes an interesting vegetarian 'burger'. Serve in a burger bun with salad, or with other vegetables. Although this dish is included as a main meal, you could omit the garlic and serve the burgers with tomatoes and vegetarian rashers for an interesting breakfast.

450 g/1 lb potatoes, cooked and mashed
225 g/8 oz cabbage, finely shredded and cooked
15 g/½ oz butter or vegan margarine*
salt and pepper
1 tablespoon olive oil
100 g/4 oz mushrooms, finely chopped
1 garlic clove, crushed

For the coating:
50 g/2 oz fine wholemeal breadcrumbs
15 g/½ oz sesame seeds or chopped mixed nuts
1 egg, beaten, or 1 tablespoon soya flour mixed with 2 tablespoons water*

■ Preheat the oven to 190°C/375°F/Gas Mark 5.
■ Mix the mashed potato and cabbage together with the butter or vegan margarine* and season to taste with salt and pepper. Allow to cool.
■ Heat the oil in a small pan and fry the mushrooms and garlic for 5 minutes. Allow to cool.
■ Take 1 heaped tablespoon of the potato and cabbage mixture in your hand and put 1 teaspoon garlic mushrooms in the centre. Top with more of the potato mixture and gently shape into a patty, enclosing the mushrooms. Repeat until the mixture is used up – it should make 8 patties. Place on a lightly floured plate and chill.
■ Mix the breadcrumbs and sesame seeds or nuts in a shallow dish. Dip each patty into beaten egg or soya paste*, and then roll to coat in the breadcrumbs.
■ Place on a greased baking sheet and bake in the preheated oven for about 35–40 minutes, turning once, until golden.

Makes 8 patties

FARFALLE WITH MANGE TOUT, FLAGEOLET BEANS, COURGETTES AND MINT

This simple meal is an excellent combination of proteins from the pasta (grain) and flageolet beans (pulse). It is fresh and light in flavour and makes a good summertime meal.

350 g/12 oz farfalle pasta

175 g/6 oz mange tout, trimmed and shredded diagonally

400 g/14 oz can chopped tomatoes

175 g/6 oz courgettes, diced

400-g/14-oz can of flageolet beans, drained

3 tablespoons chopped mint

salt and freshly ground black pepper

150 g/5 oz low-fat mozzarella cheese, cubed (omit for vegan*)

50 g/2 oz stoned olives, chopped

garlic bread, to serve (optional)

PER SERVING
■
263 kcals (1297 kj)
Protein 20 g
Fat 10.5 g
Carbohydrate 35.5 g
Fibre 4 g

■ Cook the pasta in a pan of boiling, lightly salted water, according to the instructions on the packet, until just tender and al dente. Drain and keep warm.

■ Steam the mange tout for 2 minutes and then drain and refresh under cold running water.

■ Drain the canned tomatoes and place in a saucepan with the courgettes and cook gently for 5 minutes. Stir in the mange tout and flageolet beans and heat through.

■ Add the cooked pasta and mozzarella, if using, then mix well and season to taste. Turn into a serving dish and sprinkle the chopped olives over the top. Serve with crusty garlic bread, if liked.

Serves 4

PENNE WITH
BROCCOLI, AVOCADO
AND ROAST PEPPER

PER SERVING

■

317 kcals (1320 kj)
Protein 8 g
Fat 20 g
Carbohydrate 27.5 g
Fibre 5 g

Pasta has a high fibre and protein content, and whereas avocado is high in fat it is also a good source of vitamin C. This recipe is quick and easy to prepare, making it perfect for a weekday meal.

350 g/12 oz penne pasta
225 g/8 oz broccoli, trimmed and
    separated into florets
1 red pepper, quartered and
    deseeded
1 small onion, finely chopped
1 tablespoon olive oil
1 tablespoon tarragon vinegar
1 tablespoon shoyu

4 gherkins, finely chopped
12 olives, stoned and halved
1 tablespoon chopped fresh
    coriander
1 tablespoon vegan pesto
1 avocado, peeled, stoned and sliced
25 g/1 oz pine nuts
salt and pepper
sprigs of coriander, to garnish

■ Cook the pasta in boiling water, according to the instructions on the packet, until just tender and al dente. Drain and keep warm.
■ Meanwhile, steam the broccoli florets for 6–8 minutes, and grill the red pepper, skin-side up, until blackened. Peel and then slice the flesh.
■ Gently fry the onion in the olive oil until soft and transluscent. Stir in the vinegar, shoyu, gherkins, olives, coriander and pesto. Add the broccoli, red pepper, avocado and pine nuts. Season to taste with salt and pepper. Mix well to coat and reheat gently for 2–3 minutes.
■ Stir in the hot pasta and transfer to a serving dish. Garnish with sprigs of coriander and serve immediately.

Serves 4

Opposite: Penne with broccoli, avocado and roast pepper

VEGAN

Asparagus
FETTUCCINE STIR-FRY WITH PEANUT SAUCE

Asparagus is high in vitamin C and beta-carotene. Although you can buy imported asparagus for much of the year, it is at its best during the early summer when it is in season.

PER SERVING
■
295 kcals (1230 kj)
Protein 11 g
Fat 16 g
Carbohydrate 27 g
Fibre 5 g

350 g/12 oz fettuccine pasta
225 g/8 oz asparagus, trimmed and cut into 2.5-cm/1-in pieces
225 g/8 oz thin green beans, cut into 2.5-cm/1-in pieces
1 tablespoon groundnut oil
1 large red chilli, deseeded and finely chopped
1 garlic clove, chopped
2.5-cm/1-in fresh root ginger, peeled and chopped

4 spring onions, chopped
2 tablespoons water
2 tablespoons shoyu
2 tablespoons crunchy peanut butter
15 g/½ oz basil leaves, torn
1 tablespoon toasted sesame oil
25 g/1 oz plain peanuts, roasted and chopped
extra basil leaves, to garnish

■ Cook the pasta in a large pan of boiling, lightly salted water, according to the instructions on the packet, until just tender and al dente. Drain and keep warm.

■ Steam the asparagus and green beans for 5 minutes.

■ Heat the oil in a wok and quickly fry the chilli, garlic, ginger and spring onions for 1 minute. Add the asparagus and green beans, mix well and cook for 2 minutes.

■ Cream the water, shoyu and peanut butter together and stir into the vegetables with the basil and sesame oil. Add the warm pasta and toss well to combine. Turn into a serving dish and sprinkle with the peanuts. Garnish with basil leaves and serve.

Serves 4

MILLET PILAF

VEGAN

Usually a pilaf will be made with rice, but millet works very well as a substitute and adds variety to your diet. Broad beans are in season from late spring to early summer, but frozen broad beans are also excellent, making this a tasty all-year-round dish.

1 tablespoon olive oil
1 large onion, chopped
175 g/6 oz millet
2 teaspoons ground coriander
good pinch of ground cardamom
600 ml/1 pint vegetable stock
225 g/8 oz broccoli, separated into florets
100 g/4 oz sweetcorn kernels
100 g/4 oz broad beans, cooked
50 g/2 oz sultanas
salt and freshly ground black pepper
2 teaspoons grated orange zest
2 teaspoons chopped chives or spring onions
25 g/1 oz flaked almonds, toasted

■ In a large saucepan, heat the olive oil over a medium heat and fry the onion for 5 minutes. Add the millet, coriander and cardamom. Stir and cook for 1 minute.

■ Add the stock, bring to the boil, then reduce the heat and simmer, covered, for 20 minutes.

■ Add the broccoli and cook for 5 minutes before adding the sweetcorn, broad beans, grated orange zest and sultanas. Stir well and then cook, covered, for a final 5 minutes.

■ Check the seasoning and serve, scattered with chives or spring onions and toasted flaked almonds.

Serves 4

PER SERVING
■
329 kcals (1380 kj)
Protein 12 g
Fat 9 g
Carbohydrate 53 g
Added sugar 2 g
Fibre 4.5 g

WILD MUSHROOM
RISOTTO

PER SERVING
■
624 kcals (2636 kj)
Protein 16 g
Fat 11 g
Carbohydrate 117 g
Fibre 1 g

This would make an excellent healthy main course for a dinner party if served with the Wild Flower and Herb Salad (see page 96) and topped with Onion Marmalade (see page 107). The liquid from soaking the ceps is full of flavour. It is a good idea to strain it through fine muslin before adding it to a dish as there can be a gritty residue from the mushrooms.

1 litre/1¾ pints vegetable stock
2 teaspoons olive oil
1 onion, finely chopped
350 g/12 oz arborio rice
150 ml/¼ pint dry white wine
15 g/½ oz dried ceps
15 g/½ oz vegan margarine* or butter

225 g/8 oz mixed wild mushrooms, sliced
100 g/4 oz wild rice, cooked
50 g/2 oz Camargue red wild rice, cooked
50 g/2 oz vegetarian pecorino cheese (optional – omit for vegan*)
salt and freshly ground black pepper

■ Bring the stock to the boil in a large saucepan and keep it simmering.

■ Meanwhile, heat the oil in another large saucepan and fry the onion over a low heat until soft and just starting to colour. Add the arborio rice and cook for 2 minutes, stirring all the time.

■ Pour in the wine and cook for 5 minutes. Start adding the stock, using a large ladle. Cook gently, stirring regularly and making sure that all the stock has been absorbed before adding the next ladleful. This should take about 25–30 minutes.

■ While the rice is cooking, cover the ceps with boiling water and soak for about 15–20 minutes. Drain, reserving the soaking liquid and chop.

■ Heat the butter or vegan margarine* in a frying pan and quickly cook the sliced wild mushrooms for about 5 minutes.

■ Add all the mushrooms to the rice, together with the two cooked wild rices and the reserved soaking liquid. Add a little more stock if necessary and heat through thoroughly.

■ Remove from the heat and, if using, stir in the pecorino cheese. Season to taste and serve immediately.

Serves 4

Opposite: Wild mushroom risotto with Wild flower and herb salad (page 96)

VEGETABLE AND
BLACK EYE BEAN BANGALORE

Black eye beans are one of the few pulses that don't need soaking before cooking so they are a useful store cupboard ingredient.

100 g/4 oz black eye beans
1 tablespoon vegetable oil
1 onion, sliced
100 g/4 oz carrots, sliced
100 g/4 oz potatoes, cubed, washed and dried on kitchen paper
2 green chillies, sliced
2.5-cm/1-in piece of cinnamon stick
6 whole cloves
6 green cardamons
2 teaspoons cumin seeds
1 teaspoon ground cumin
1 teaspoon ground coriander
¼ teaspoon turmeric
2.5-cm/1-in fresh root ginger, peeled and grated
1 bay leaf
100 g/4 oz thin green beans, sliced
100 g/4 oz courgettes, sliced
175 ml/6 fl oz water
100 g/4 oz pineapple, peeled and cut into cubes
1 banana, sliced
salt, to taste
150 ml/5 fl oz natural low-fat yogurt or soya yogurt*
fresh coriander leaves, to garnish

■ Place the dry black eye beans in a saucepan. Cover with water, bring to the boil and then simmer for about 30 minutes or until the beans are tender. Drain.

■ Heat the oil in a large saucepan and fry the onion, carrots, potatoes and chillies for 5 minutes, stirring. Add all the spices and the ginger and cook for a further 2 minutes.

■ Add the bay leaf, green beans, courgettes and water. Cover and cook until the vegetables are tender (about 15 minutes).

■ Add the pineapple, banana, black eye beans and yogurt and gently heat through. Season to taste with salt and serve on a bed of rice, garnished with coriander leaves.

Serves 4

Mushroom, Pepper
AND TOMATO STEW
WITH QUINOA

Quinoa is an excellent source of protein. It is an ancient grain which has recently regained popularity in the West and makes a good alternative to bulgar wheat or cous cous.

PER SERVING

■

313 kcals (1319 kj)
Protein 15 g
Fat 7 g
Carbohydrate 50 g
Fibre 4 g

1 tablespoon vegetable oil

225 g/8 oz baby onions or shallots, halved

675 g/1½ lb mixed mushrooms (button, oyster, chestnut, etc.), wiped and quartered if large

2 garlic cloves, chopped

sprig of rosemary

3 tablespoons shoyu

25 g/1 oz dark muscovado sugar

2 teaspoons yeast extract

300 ml/½ pint vegetable stock

1 red pepper, deseeded and cut into thin strips

400-g/14-oz can of chopped tomatoes

salt and freshly ground black pepper

2 teaspoons arrowroot

225 g/8 oz quinoa, cooked and kept warm

handful of chopped parsley, to garnish

■ Heat the oil in a large saucepan and fry the onions until starting to brown. Stir in the mushrooms, garlic and sprig of rosemary and cook over a high heat until the mushrooms start to release their juices.

■ In a bowl, mix together the shoyu, sugar and yeast extract, which has been dissolved in the stock. Season well and add to the mushroooms with the red pepper and tomatoes. Simmer for 20–30 minutes until half of the liquid has evaporated.

■ In a small bowl or cup, mix the arrowroot with a little water to make a paste. Add to the stew, then bring to the boil, stirring. Reduce the heat and simmer for 1 minute to thicken. Remove the sprig of rosemary and check the seasoning.

■ Put the cooked quinoa on a serving platter and spoon the stew over the top. Sprinkle with lots of chopped parsley and serve.

Serves 4

NUTTY FLAN WITH
TOFU AND VEGETABLE FILLING

Tofu can be used as a substitute for cream and eggs in flans. This recipe is good if you don't like making pastry as no rolling out is involved. To make a vegan version, omit the cheese and oil from the flan case and use 50 g/2 oz vegan margarine rubbed into the mixture. It will be more crumbly than the cheese version, but still tasty.

PER SERVING
■
389 kcals (1620 kj)
Protein 16 g
Carbohydrate 24 g
Fat 26 g
Fibre 5 g

Flan case:
50 g/2 oz ground almonds
50 g/2 oz low-fat vegetarian
    Cheddar cheese, finely grated
50 g/2 oz wholemeal breadcrumbs
25 g/1 oz chopped roast hazelnuts
1 teaspoon dried mixed herbs
¼ teaspoon cayenne pepper
    (optional)
2 tablespoons groundnut oil

Filling:
2 onions, cut into bite-sized chunks
100 g/4 oz carrots, sliced into
    2.5-cm/1-in lengths

1 red pepper, deseeded and chopped
    into 2.5-cm/1-in pieces
100 g/4 oz sweet potato, chopped
    into 2.5-cm/1-in cubes
1 tablespoon olive oil
200 g/7 oz silken tofu
1 tablespoon cider vinegar
1 teaspoon each of dried rosemary,
    sage and thyme, ground together
    in a pestle and mortar
150 ml/¼ pint skimmed or soya milk
salt and freshly ground black pepper
1 tablespoon sunflower seeds

■ Preheat the oven to 200°C/400°F/Gas Mark 6.
■ Mix all the ingredients for the flan case together and press into a 17-cm/7-in loose-bottomed flan ring. Bake in the preheated oven for 10 minutes.
■ Put all the vegetables in a roasting pan, drizzle the oil over and toss well. Roast in the preheated oven for about 30–40 minutes, turning several times, until tender and golden.
■ Put the tofu, cider vinegar, dried herbs and milk into a blender or food processor and blend until smooth. Season well.
■ Put the roast vegetables in the flan case, then spoon the tofu mixture evenly over the top. Sprinkle sunflower seeds over the surface and bake for 20–25 minutes.
■ Turn out onto a serving plate and serve with a green salad or seasonal vegetables.

Serves 6

Opposite: Nutty flan with tofu and vegetable filling

SWEET AND SOUR
CABBAGE PARCELS

PER SERVING
■
194 kcals (806 kj)
Protein 5 g
Fat 11 g
Carbohydrate 20 g
Added sugar 3 g
Fibre 5 g

Tying up the cabbage leaves with chives makes this nutritious dish look like little Christmas parcels.

4 large leaves from a Savoy cabbage
1 tablespoon olive oil
1 small onion, finely chopped
1 garlic clove, crushed
100 g/4 oz mushrooms, chopped
25 g/1 oz toasted pine kernels
1 teaspoon wholegrain mustard
1 tablespoon shoyu or tamari sauce
pinch of dried sage and thyme
salt and freshly ground black pepper
long chives
a little vegetable stock

Sweet and sour peppers:
1 tablespoon olive oil
1 large onion, cut in half and thinly sliced
2 garlic cloves, crushed
2 red peppers, deseeded and shredded into long thin strips
2 yellow peppers, deseeded and shredded into long thin strips
200-g/7-oz can of chopped tomatoes
1 tablespoon tomato purée
2 tablespoons cider vinegar
1 tablespoon honey or maple syrup*
1 tablespoon balsamic vinegar
salt and freshly ground black pepper

■ Preheat the oven to 180°C/350°F/Gas Mark 4. Remove the base of the stem from each cabbage leaf, and blanch the leaves for 4–5 minutes to soften.

■ Heat the oil in a saucepan and fry the onion and garlic for a few minutes until starting to colour. Add the mushrooms and cook gently for 5 minutes. Stir in the pine kernels, mustard, shoyu or tamari, sage, thyme and seasoning.

■ Divide the mixture between the cabbage leaves and roll up tightly, tucking in the sides. Use chives to tie each one (criss-cross style) to look like a parcel.

■ Place in an ovenproof dish, add a little vegetable stock, cover with foil and bake in the preheated oven for 45–50 minutes.

■ Meanwhile, heat the oil and fry the onion, garlic and peppers for 5 minutes until softening. Add the tomatoes, tomato purée, cider vinegar and honey or maple syrup*, and bring to the boil. Remove from the heat, add the balsamic vinegar and season. Remove half of the mixture with a slotted spoon and reserve. Blend the remaining mixture, with all the juices, to a smooth sauce.

■ Gently reheat the reserved peppers and the sauce in separate saucepans. Put a mound of the pepper mixture on each warm serving plate. Place a cabbage parcel on top, then drizzle the pepper sauce on the plate around it.

Serves 4

ENCHILADAS WITH
WARM TOMATO SALSA

VEGAN

If you can't get black beans, kidney beans or pinto beans work well in this Mexican-style dish.

1 tablespoon groundnut oil

1 onion, halved and sliced

1 red chilli, finely chopped

1 teaspoon ground coriander

100 g/4 oz black beans, cooked

100 g/4 oz sweetcorn kernels
   (defrosted if using frozen)

1 tablespoon chopped fresh
   coriander

juice of 1 lime

salt and freshly ground black pepper

4 large soft flour tortillas

For the salsa:

1 tablespoon tomato purée

4 tablespoons water

1 small red onion, finely chopped

1 garlic clove, crushed

4 ripe tomatoes, roughly chopped

1 tablespoon chopped fresh
   coriander

PER SERVING
■

255 kcals (1081 kj)
Protein 10.5 g
Fat 4 g
Carbohydrate 47 g
Fibre 6 g

■ Preheat the oven to 180°C/350°F/Gas Mark 4.

■ Heat the oil and fry the onion and chilli until tender. Add the ground coriander and cook for 2 minutes. Stir in the cooked black beans, sweetcorn, coriander and lime juice and stir thoroughly to heat through. Season to taste and keep warm.

■ Wrap the tortillas in foil and warm through in the preheated oven for 10 minutes.

■ To make the salsa, put the tomato purée and water in a small saucepan with the onion and garlic. Stir and cook for 10 minutes. Add the chopped tomatoes and coriander and mix well. Remove from the heat.

■ Divide the filling between the 4 tortillas and fold each one over in half to make a semicircular shape. Spoon the warm salsa over the top of each and serve with a green salad.

Serves 4

PER SERVING
■

494 kcals (2077 kj)
Protein 28 g
Fat 17 g
Carbohydrate 60 g
Fibre 4 g

SZECHUAN TOFU

Szechuan (Sichuan) pepper, although hot and spicy, is not really a variety of pepper at all but the dried berries and husks from a type of ash tree. It is one of the ingredients in Chinese five-spice powder.

225 g/8 oz long-grain rice
2 teaspoons groundnut oil
1 garlic clove, peeled
2.5-cm/1-in piece fresh root ginger, peeled
2 dried red chillies
1 tablespoon szechuan peppercorns
1 onion, chopped
1 green pepper, sliced
225 g/8 oz marinated tofu pieces
225 g/8 oz mushrooms, sliced
225 g/8 oz broccoli florets
2 tablespoons vegetable stock
2 tablespoons shoyu
50 g/2 oz cashew nuts, toasted

■ Cook the rice, according to the packet instructions, and keep warm if necessary.

■ Heat the oil in a wok. Use a rolling pin to bruise the garlic and ginger. When the oil is hot, add the garlic, ginger and chillies and allow to sizzle for 5 minutes. Remove with a slotted spoon and discard.

■ Meanwhile, dry-roast the szechuan peppercorns and grind in a pestle and mortar or grinder attachment. Add to the wok with the onion and green pepper and cook for 5 minutes. Add the tofu, mushrooms and broccoli and cook for 5 minutes, then add the stock and shoyu and allow to simmer for 5–10 minutes until the vegetables are tender but still crisp.

■ Stir in the toasted cashew nuts and serve on a bed of rice.

Serves 4

Opposite: Szechuan tofu

MARINATED TOFU
AND VEGETABLE FILO PIE

Tofu is a versatile ingredient and in addition to being one of the best vegetarian protein sources it also gives substance to a meal.

PER SERVING
■

355 kcals (1483 kj)
Protein 22 g
Fat 15 g
Carbohydrate 34 g
Added sugar 0.6 g
Fibre 5 g

1 teaspoon olive oil
100 g/4 oz leeks, trimmed and sliced
1 garlic clove, crushed
pinch of chilli powder
100 g/4 oz carrots, diced
100 g/4 oz parsnips, diced
100 g/4 oz swede, diced
100 g/4 oz thin green beans, frozen
225 g/8 oz marinated tofu pieces
100 g/4 oz tomatoes, skinned and chopped
1 tablespoon tomato purée
300 ml/½ pint vegetable stock
salt and pepper
1 tablespoon plain white flour
3 sheets filo pastry, or 100 g/4 oz depending on the size of sheet
15 g/½ oz vegan margarine, melted

■ Preheat the oven to 200°C/400°F/Gas Mark 6.
■ Heat the oil in a large saucepan and sweat the leeks and garlic together, with the lid on, for 5 minutes. Add the chilli powder, carrots, parsnips, swede and green beans and cook gently for 10 minutes.
■ Add the tofu pieces, tomatoes, tomato purée and vegetable stock and cook gently until the vegetables are tender. Season well. Sprinkle the flour over and stir to mix. Cool and transfer to a pie dish.
■ Brush one sheet of filo pastry with melted margarine and place over the vegetables. Trim to size. Repeat with the remaining 2 sheets. Scrunch up the pastry trimmings roughly and scatter over the top. Bake in the preheated oven for 20 minutes until golden. Serve immediately.

Serves 4

BROAD BEAN AND
SWEETCORN STEW

VEGAN

Stews are usually associated with winter but this one uses summer vegetables. However, you could substitute frozen vegetables when fresh ones are out of season. Bulgar wheat gives the stew bulk.

1 teaspoon olive oil

1 onion, chopped

1 red chilli, finely chopped

1 tablespoon fresh oregano

400-g/14-oz can of chopped tomatoes

450 g/1 lb broad beans (shelled weight)

225 g/8 oz sweetcorn kernels

225 g/8 oz carrots, sliced

450 ml/15 fl oz vegetable stock

100 g/4 oz bulgar wheat

grated zest and juice of 1 lemon

salt and freshly ground black pepper

2 tablespoons chopped parsley

jacket potatoes and a fresh green salad, to serve

PER SERVING
■
565 kcals (2369 kj)
Protein 20 g
Fat 7 g
Carbohydrate 109 g
Added sugar 4 g
Fibre 10 g

■ Heat the oil in a large saucepan and cook the onion, chilli and oregano until the onion has softened. Add the tomatoes, broad beans, sweetcorn, carrots and vegetable stock and bring to the boil.

■ Add the bulgar wheat and simmer for about 15–20 minutes until the vegetables and bulgar wheat are cooked. Stir in the lemon juice and zest.

■ Season to taste with salt and pepper and sprinkle with chopped parsley. Serve with jacket potatoes and a green salad.

Serves 4

PATATAS BRAVAS

PER SERVING
■

163 kcals (686 kj)
Protein 4 g
Fat 3 g
Carbohydrate 31 g
Fibre 3 g

Potatoes and parsley are both good sources of vitamin C. This spicy combination makes a good side dish.

1 tablespoon groundnut oil
675 g/1½ lb cooked cubed potatoes
1 onion, finely chopped
1 teaspoon chilli powder

2–3 tablespoons tomato purée
1 tablespoon chopped parsley, to garnish

■ Heat the oil in a non-stick frying pan. Gently fry the potatoes, onion and chilli powder together for about 10 minutes until the vegetables are golden. Stir in the tomato purée.
■ Serve the potatoes as a side dish, garnished with chopped parsley.

Serves 4

SPICED RED CABBAGE

PER SERVING
■

72 kcals (299 kj)
Protein 2 g
Fat 3 g
Carbohydrate 9 g
Fibre 4 g

Sunflower oil is lighter in flavour than olive oil, is high in polyunsaturates and a good source of vitamin E.

1 tablespoon sunflower oil
1 onion, chopped
450 g/1 lb red cabbage, shredded
225 g/8 oz cooking apples, peeled, cored and diced

2.5-cm/1-in piece fresh root ginger, peeled and grated
pinch of ground cinnamon or allspice
150 ml/¼ pint vegetable stock
salt and freshly ground black pepper

■ Heat the oil in a large saucepan. Add the onion, red cabbage and apple and cook gently for 5 minutes. Add the ginger and cinnamon or allspice and the vegetable stock.
■ Bring to the boil, then reduce the heat and simmer gently for 15–20 minutes until most of the liquid has evaporated and the vegetables are tender. Season to taste and serve.

Serves 4 as a side dish

Opposite: Patatas Bravas and Spiced red cabbage

QUICK-FRIED
SHREDDED KOHLRABI

Kohlrabi looks so strange that it can be difficult to think what to do with it! However, this unusual vegetable can be sliced and boiled like a turnip or stir-fried with other flavoursome ingredients.

1 tablespoon vegetable oil
225 g/8 oz kohlrabi, peeled and grated
1 onion, halved and sliced
2.5-cm/1-in piece fresh root ginger, peeled and grated
dash of Tabasco
salt and freshly ground black pepper

■ Heat the oil in a non-stick frying pan. Gently fry the kohlrabi and onion for about 10 minutes until tender. Add the ginger and stir well to warm through.
■ Season with Tabasco and salt and pepper to taste and serve immediately.

Serves 4 as a side dish

SWEET BAKED
BEETROOT

Beetroot is high in Vitamins A, C and K, and also in the minerals iron and calcium. This is a delicious way to prepare this often forgotten vegetable.

675 g/1½ lb raw beetroot, peeled and quartered
2 red onions, peeled and quartered
2 tablespoons olive oil
1 tablespoon honey or maple syrup*
salt and freshly ground black pepper
1 tablespoon balsamic vinegar

■ Preheat the oven to 180°C/350°F/Gas Mark 4.
■ Place the beetroot and onion quarters in a roasting pan.
■ Mix the olive oil and honey or maple syrup* together and season well. Pour over the vegetables and toss to coat.
■ Roast in the preheated oven for about 45–60 minutes until the beetroot is tender. Sprinkle with the balsamic vinegar and toss well. Serve immediately.

Serves 4 as a side dish

CELERIAC MASH

A warming, starchy side dish. If you want to reduce the fat content, use less (or no) margarine when mashing the mixture.

450 g/1 lb potatoes, peeled and cubed
450 g/1 lb celeriac, peeled and cubed
50 g/2 oz vegan margarine
2 sticks celery, very finely chopped
2 garlic cloves, crushed
2 tablespoons fresh basil or coriander, chopped
salt and pepper

PER SERVING
■
203 kcals (848 kj)
Protein 4 g
Fat 11 g
Carbohydrate 23 g
Fibre 6 g

■ Boil the potato and celeriac together until tender. Drain and mash.
■ Meanwhile, heat the margarine in a frying pan and gently cook the celery and garlic until tender. Stir into the mashed potato, add the herbs and season.

Serves 4

TERIYAKI STIR-FRY

T eriyaki sauce contains honey so it is not suitable for a vegan diet, but you could use the tempeh marinade on page 94 instead.

225 g/8 oz egg-free noodles
1 tablespoon groundnut oil
1 onion, sliced
1 garlic clove, crushed
100 g/4 oz broccoli florets
100 g/4 oz asparagus spears, cut into 2.5-cm/1-in lengths and steamed
50 g/2 oz baby sweetcorn, halved
50 g/2 oz mange tout, trimmed and halved
100 g/4 oz thin green beans, cut into 2.5-cm/1-in lengths
175 g/6 oz beansprouts
3 tablespoons teriyaki sauce
100 g/4 oz cherry tomatoes, halved

PER SERVING
■
117 kcals (490 kj)
Protein 7 g
Fat 4 g
Carbohydrate 15 g
Fibre 3 g

■ Cook the noodles, according to the instructions on the packet. Drain and keep warm.
■ Heat the oil in a wok. Add the onion and garlic and cook for 2 minutes. Add the broccoli and cauliflower and cook for 6 minutes. Add the asparagus, sweetcorn, mange tout and green beans and continue stir-frying for 3 minutes.
■ Stir in the beansprouts and teriyaki sauce and serve on a bed of noodles, garnished with the cherry tomatoes.

Serves 4

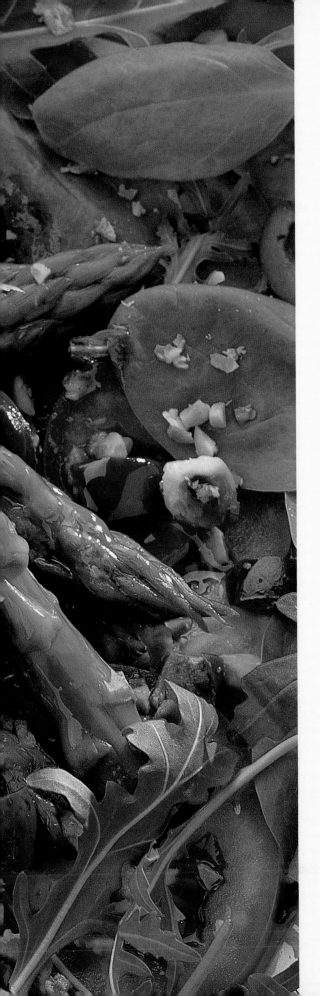

SALADS,
DRESSINGS AND RELISHES

Mixed grain tabbouleh salad
Sprouting bean salad with ginger dressing
Apricot and chick pea salad
Spicy bean salad
Mixed potato salad
Japanese sea vegetable salad
Beetroot salad with toasted seeds
Rice noodle salad with oriental vegetables
Marinated tempeh and baby vegetable salad
  with tofu mayonnaise
Wild flower and herb salad
Italian grilled pepper salad
Asparagus salad with hazelnut dressing
Mixed green salad with tofu and mango
Walnut dressing
Spinach and mint salad with garlic croutons
Thai tofu dip
Sun-dried tomato dip
Teriyaki dressing
Sweetcorn salsa
Cucumber, apple, onion and mint relish
Banana, onion and tomato chutney
Fresh orange and date chutney
Courgette relish
Onion marmalade

Left: Asparagus salad with hazelnut dressing (page 98)

MIXED GRAIN
TABBOULEH SALAD

PER SERVING

■

149 kcals (620 kj)
Protein 3 g
Fat 8 g
Carbohydrate 17 g
Fibre 2 g

Using a mixture of grains gives variety of texture and flavour to this popular salad. If you wish to make it healthier still, reduce the amount of olive oil and substitute a little more lemon juice.

50 g/2 oz millet, cooked
50 g/2 oz bulgar wheat, cooked
½ green pepper, deseeded and finely diced
½ red pepper, finely diced
½ carrot, very finely diced
6 spring onions, finely chopped
¼ cucumber, very finely diced
2 tomatoes, skinned and finely diced
4 tablespoons fruity olive oil
1 garlic clove, crushed
3 tablespoons lemon juice
2 tablespoons chopped parsley
2 tablespoons chopped mint
salt and freshly ground black pepper

■ Combine the two cooked grains in a bowl and mix in the peppers, carrot, spring onions, cucumber and tomatoes.
■ In a separate bowl, mix the olive oil, garlic, lemon juice, parsley and mint and season to taste.
■ Pour over the salad ingredients and mix well. Chill in the refrigerator before serving.

Serves 6

SPROUTING
BEAN SALAD WITH GINGER DRESSING

When beans and seeds are sprouting, they are at their most nutritious and are an excellent ingredient to include in your diet, either raw or stir-fried. Chick peas, mung beans, aduki beans, alfalfa and fenugreek seeds make an interesting mixture and you can sprout them in a jam jar in a few days so that you have an almost constant and inexpensive supply of them.

225 g/8 oz mixed sprouting beans
1 red pepper, deseeded and finely sliced
1 stick celery, shredded
1 red onion, finely sliced
¼ cucumber, quartered, then sliced
50 g/2 oz watercress, washed and chopped

Ginger dressing:
5-cm/2-in piece fresh root ginger, grated and juice squeezed out
1 tablespoon shoyu
juice of 1 lime
1 garlic clove, crushed
salt and pepper to taste

■ Mix all the salad ingredients together in a bowl.
■ Make the dressing by mixing the ginger juice, shoyu, lime juice and garlic together. Season to taste.
■ Pour the dressing over the salad, toss well and serve immediately.

Serves 4

PER SERVING
■
48 kcals (201 kj)
Protein 3 g
Fat 0.7 g
Carbohydrate 8 g
Fibre 2 g

APRICOT AND
CHICK PEA SALAD

PER SERVING
■
483 kcals (2021 kJ)
Protein 14 g
Fat 9 g
Carbohydrate 88 g
Fibre 3 g

D ried apricots are a good source of iron and their flavour complements the slight earthiness of the chick peas to make a delicious and unusual salad. Served with cubes of grilled smoked tofu, this would make a good light lunch.

100 g/4 oz bulgar wheat
100 g/4 oz cooked chick peas
50 g/2 oz sprouted chick peas/mixed
   beansprouts
50 g/2 oz ready-to-eat apricots,
   chopped
25 g/1 oz toasted, flaked almonds
2 tablespoons chopped parsley
sprigs of parsley, to garnish

Dressing:
1 tablespoon groundnut oil
1 small onion, finely chopped
1 teaspoon crushed dried chillies
1 teaspoon ground cumin
pinch ground cinnamon
pinch ground cloves
salt and pepper

■ Pour boiling water over the bulgar wheat and leave to stand for 30 minutes, then drain. Fluff up the grains with a fork.

■ Mix together the bulgar wheat, chick peas, sprouted chick peas, apricots, almonds and parsley in a bowl.

■ To make the dressing, heat the oil in a saucepan and fry the onion until soft. Add the spices and cook for 2 minutes. Season to taste and stir into the salad immediately while the dressing is still warm. Garnish with sprigs of parsley and serve.

Serves 4

Opposite: Apricot and chick pea salad

SPICY BEAN SALAD

A spicy variation on the traditional three-bean salad, this dish is very high in protein.

1 teaspoon vegetable oil
1 onion, finely chopped
2 teaspoons garam masala
½ teaspoon chilli powder
400-g/14-oz can of kidney beans, rinsed and drained

400-g/14-oz can of butterbeans, rinsed and drained
175 g/6 oz thin green beans, cooked
crisp lettuce leaves, shredded, to serve

■ Heat the oil in a saucepan and fry the onion until soft. Add the garam masala and chilli powder and cook for 2 minutes.
■ Add all the beans and heat through, stirring to coat. Remove from the heat and cool.
■ Serve on a bed of shredded crisp lettuce leaves.

Serves 4

MIXED POTATO SALAD

This salad is high in starchy carbohydrate and makes an excellent side dish in both summer and winter.

375 g/12 oz potatoes, cubed
375 g/12 oz sweet potatoes, cubed
100 g/4 oz green beans
1 small red onion, finely sliced
3 ripe tomatoes, skinned and chopped

1 tablespoon fruity olive oil
1 tablespoon lemon juice
1 tablespoon chopped oregano
salt and freshly ground black pepper

■ Cook the potatoes and sweet potatoes in a pan of boiling water until tender. Drain.
■ Cook the green beans in boiling water, then drain and add to the potatoes with the onion and tomatoes.
■ Mix the olive oil, lemon juice and oregano together. Season to taste and pour over the salad while still warm. Put into a salad bowl and serve.

Serves 4

JAPANESE SEA
VEGETABLE SALAD

Sea vegetables are full of vitamins and minerals, but in most recipes you need only use a tiny pinch as once soaked they expand to four or five times their original volume.

pinch of dried arame or hiziki

225 g/8 oz beansprouts, washed and drained

½ cucumber, halved lengthways and finely sliced

50 g/2 oz mange tout, trimmed and shredded

50 g/2 oz carrots, cut into long thin strips

4 tablespoons rice vinegar

I tablespoon shoyu

I teaspoon caster sugar

¼–½ teaspoon wasabi (Japanese horseradish)

pinch of salt

I tablespoon sesame seeds, dry toasted

PER SERVING
■

57 kcals (239 kj)
Protein 3.5 g
Fat 2 g
Carbohydrate 7 g
Fibre 2 g

■ Soak the arame or hiziki in cold water for 10 minutes to reconstitute. Drain.

■ Mix the arame, beansprouts, cucumber, mange tout and carrots together in a bowl.

■ Mix together the rice vinegar, shoyu, caster sugar, wasabi paste and salt, and pour over the salad just before serving. Toss all the ingredients together in the bowl, then sprinkle toasted sesame seeds over the top to garnish.

Serves 4

BEETROOT SALAD
WITH TOASTED SEEDS

VEGAN

PER SERVING
■
131 kcals (543 kj)
Protein 4 g
Fat 9.5 g
Carbohydrate 7.5 g
Fibre 3 g

If you want to cut down on the fat in your diet, you could try reducing the fat in this recipe to 1 teaspoon sesame oil to give just a hint of its distinctive flavour in the dressing.

225 g/8 oz raw beetroot, grated
6 spring onions, shredded
2 sticks celery, shredded
50 g/2 oz baby spinach leaves
1 tablespoon pumpkin seeds
1 tablespoon sunflower seeds
1 tablespoon sesame seeds

For the dressing:
2 tablespoons red wine vinegar
1 tablespoon sesame oil
2 teaspoons groundnut oil
1 tablespoon shoyu or tamari
1 tablespoon chopped mint
salt and pepper

■ Make the dressing by stirring all the ingredients together.
■ Mix the grated beetroot, spring onions and celery together in a bowl and pour the dressing over, mixing well to coat.
■ Arrange the spinach leaves on a serving platter, then pile the beetroot mixture on top, leaving a border of spinach leaves showing.
■ In a heavy-based, non-stick pan, dry-roast the seeds until golden and popping. Scatter over the salad and serve.

Serves 4

RICE NOODLE SALAD
WITH ORIENTAL VEGETABLES

A low fat salad, with quickly stir-fried vegetables to preserve the nutritional content.

50 g/2 oz rice noodles

1 tablespoon groundnut oil

25 g/1 oz baby sweetcorn halved

25 g/1 oz mange tout, trimmed and sliced diagonally

3 spring onions, shredded diagonally

5-cm/2-in piece daikon, peeled and grated

25 g/1 oz shitake mushrooms, sliced

1 quantity of Teriyaki Dressing (see page 103)

pinch of arame, soaked and drained

25 g/1 oz peanuts, roasted and chopped, to garnish

■ Cook the rice noodles according to the instructions on the packet. Drain and plunge immediately into cold water. When cold, drain. Chop into shorter lengths if preferred and place in a bowl.

■ Heat the oil in a frying pan and quickly stir-fry all the vegetables for 2–3 minutes. Remove from the heat.

■ Add the teriyaki dressing while the vegetables are still warm. Pour over the rice noodles and immediately toss well to coat. Leave to cool and add the arame.

■ Arrange on a serving platter and scatter the peanuts over the top. Allow to cool and serve.

Serves 4

PER SERVING (EXCLUDING TERIYAKI DRESSING)
■
109 kcals (454 kj)
Protein 3 g
Fat 6 g
Carbohydrate 12 g
Fibre 1 g

MARINATED TEMPEH
AND BABY VEGETABLE SALAD WITH TOFU MAYONNAISE

PER SERVING
■

147 kcals (609 kj)
Protein 8 g
Fat 11 g
Carbohydrate 5 g
Fibre 2 g

VARIATIONS
■

Add one of the following
flavourings to the tofu
mayonnaise in place of
the coriander:

■ 1 tablespoon chopped
mixed herbs
■ 1 tablespoon
vegetarian or vegan pesto
■ 2 tablespoons
Sun-dried Tomato Dip
(see page 103)
■ 1 heaped teaspoon
capers and 1 large
gherkin, finely chopped
■ 1 tablespoon sweet
fruit chutney (e.g. mango,
peach)
■ 1 teaspoon curry paste

You can buy tempeh in the freezer section of health food shops or it is sometimes bottled in brine. Tempeh is a good source of protein as it is made from soya beans.

100 g/4 oz tempeh, defrosted
2 tablespoons shoyu or tamari
1 garlic clove, crushed
1 tablespoon groundnut oil
50 g/2 oz baby carrots, sliced
   lenthways
50 g/2 oz baby sweetcorn, halved
   lenthways
25 g/1 oz petit pois (frozen)
100 g/4 oz Chinese leaves, shredded

Tofu mayonnaise:
50 g/2 oz silken tofu
1 garlic clove, crushed
grated zest and juice of ½ lemon
2 tablespoons cold pressed
   sunflower oil
2 tablespoons water
15 g/½ oz fresh coriander, chopped
salt and freshly ground black pepper

■ Slice the tempeh into thin strips about 2.5 cm/1 in long.
■ Mix the shoyu or tamari with the garlic and toss the tempeh in the mixture. Leave to marinate for 30–60 minutes.
■ Remove the tempeh from the marinade with a slotted spoon. Toss in the oil, then cook under a medium grill for about 10 minutes until golden. Cool.
■ Meanwhile, steam the baby carrots and sweetcorn for 6–10 minutes until tender. Cook the petit pois in boiling water for 2–3 minutes until tender. Drain and cool.
■ Arrange the Chinese leaves on a platter. Mix the tempeh and vegetables together and scatter over the leaves.
■ For the mayonnaise, put all the ingredients except the coriander in a blender or food processor. Blend until smooth. If too thick, add a little more water or lemon juice. If too thin, add a little more tofu. Stir in the coriander and season to taste. Drizzle over the salad and serve.

Serves 4

Opposite: Marinated tempeh and baby vegetable salad with tofu mayonnaise

VEGAN

WILD FLOWER
AND HERB SALAD

This colourful and unusual salad is best made with herbs and flowers picked fresh from the garden on which no pesticides have been used. It goes well with Wild Mushroom Risotto (see page 68).

It goes well with Wild Mushroom Risotto (see page 68).

PER SERVING
■

63 kcals (261 kj)
Protein 2 g
Fat 4.5 g
Carbohydrate 4 g
Fibre 1 g

50 g/2 oz rocket leaves
50 g/2 oz baby spinach leaves
15 g/½ oz mint leaves
15 g/½ oz flat-leaf parsley
15 g/½ oz basil, roughly torn
small bunch of chives, chopped
a few chive flowers
a few oregano flowers
1 small red onion, halved and very
    finely sliced
225 g/8 oz cherry tomatoes, halved
12 nasturtium flowers (or other
    edible flowers), to garnish

Mustard dressing:
2 teaspoons dijon mustard
2 tablespoons tarragon or other
    herb vinegar
1 garlic clove, crushed
1 tablespoon fruity extra virgin olive
    oil
finely chopped zest of 1 lemon
salt and pepper

■ Mix the rocket, spinach, mint, parsley, basil, chives and the herb flowers in a large salad bowl. Scatter over the onion and cherry tomatoes and decorate with nasturtium flowers.

■ To make the dressing, whisk all the ingredients together in a small bowl (a balloon whisk is best). Pour into a small jug and serve with the salad.

Serves 4

ITALIAN GRILLED
PEPPER SALAD

Red and yellow peppers are high in beta-carotene. Add the raw salad vegetables too and this salad is not only full of vitamins, but low in calories and fat.

PER SERVING
■

94 kcals (393 kj)
Protein 4 g
Fat 5 g
Fibre 3.5 g

1 large cos lettuce

2 red peppers

2 green peppers

2 yellow peppers

225 g/8 oz cherry tomatoes, halved

15 g/½ oz basil leaves, roughly torn

1 tablespoon capers

50 g/2 oz olives, stoned and halved

1 tablespoon fruity olive oil

grated zest of 1 lemon

1 tablespoon balsamic vinegar

pinch of salt

25 g/1 oz vegetarian Parmesan or pecorino cheese (optional – omit for vegan*)

■ Shred the lettuce and arrange on a platter.

■ Cut the peppers into quarters and remove the seeds. Grill, skin-side up, until starting to char. Cut into strips and place in a bowl. Add the cherry tomatoes, basil leaves, capers and olives.

■ Mix the olive oil, lemon zest and juice, balsamic vinegar, salt and pepper together.

■ Toss the vegetables in the dressing and arrange on the bed of lettuce. Use a cheese parer to make thin slivers of Parmesan or pecorino, if using, and scatter over the salad. Serve with rustic, crusty, Italian bread.

Serves 6

ASPARAGUS SALAD
WITH HAZELNUT DRESSING

PER SERVING
■
135 kcals (557 kj)
Protein 3 g
Fat 11 g
Carbohydrate 5 g
Fibre 3 g

Although nuts and olives are high in fat, nuts are also a good protein source and olives add interest to the flavours in your diet. You can balance this out by serving this salad with a low-fat main course such as Farfalle with Mange Tout, Flageolet Beans, Courgettes and Mint (see page 63).

225 g/8 oz asparagus spears
25 g/1 oz baby spinach leaves
25 g/1 oz rocket leaves
450 g/1 lb tomatoes, sliced
2 tablespoons fruity olive oil
2 teaspoons hazelnut oil
1 tablespoon balsamic vinegar
salt and freshly ground black pepper
25 g/1 oz stoned black olives, roughly chopped
15 g/½ oz roasted chopped hazelnuts

■ Steam the asparagus spears for 6–10 minutes. As soon as they are tender, refresh under cold running water and then cut into 5-cm/2-in lengths.
■ Arrange the spinach and rocket leaves around the edge of a serving platter. Arrange the slices of tomato in a ring inside the leaves, leaving room in the centre of the plate for the asparagus spears. Place the cooled asparagus in the centre.
■ Mix the olive oil, hazelnut oil, balsamic vinegar and salt and pepper together and drizzle over the salad. Sprinkle with the chopped olives and toasted hazelnuts and serve.

Serves 4

Opposite: Asparagus salad with hazelnut dressing

MIXED GREEN SALAD
WITH TOFU AND MANGO

Fruit is a delicious addition to many salad mixtures, and mango, in particular, goes well with tofu. Baking the tofu changes its texture and adds to the interest of the salad.

100 g/4 oz iceberg lettuce, shredded
50 g/2 oz baby spinach leaves
50 g/2 oz watercress
4 spring onions, shredded

¼ cucumber, sliced
100 g/4 oz marinated tofu
1 tablespoon sunflower oil
2 mangoes, peeled, stoned and sliced

■ Preheat the oven to 200°C/400°F/Gas Mark 6. Preheat the grill.

■ Mix the salad leaves, onions and cucumber together and arrange on a platter. Chill in the refrigerator.

■ Cut the tofu into small cubes and toss in the oil. Place on a baking sheet and bake in the preheated oven for 20–30 minutes until golden and starting to crisp.

■ Place the slices of mango under the hot grill and cook, turning once, for about 6 minutes.

■ Scatter the tofu and mango over the green salad. Serve with either Walnut Dressing (below) or Teryaki Dressing (see page 103).

Serves 4

WALNUT DRESSING

1 tablespoon cold pressed sunflower oil
1 teaspoon walnut oil
juice of 1 lemon

15 g/½ oz walnuts, lightly toasted and chopped
salt and pepper

■ Mix all the ingredients together and serve with a green salad.

Serves 4

SPINACH AND MINT
SALAD WITH GARLIC CROUTONS

*CAN BE VEGAN

Mint comes in all sorts of flavours. For this salad, I like to pick a selection of spearmint, peppermint, applemint, ginger mint and pineapple mint. You can use whatever combination you like or a single variety if you prefer.

100 g/4 oz baby spinach leaves, washed
25 g/1 oz lamb's lettuce
15 g/½ oz mint leaves, roughly chopped
100 g/4 oz cherry tomatoes (red and yellow if available), halved
15 g/½ oz pine nuts, toasted

Yogurt dressing:
75 ml/3 fl oz low-fat natural dairy or soya yoghurt*
1 tablespoon lemon or lime juice
1 teaspoon finely chopped mint
salt and pepper

Garlic croûtons:
3 slices day-old ciabatta bread
1 garlic clove, peeled and left whole

■ Toss the spinach, lamb's lettuce and mint leaves together and place in a salad bowl or serving platter. Scatter the cherry tomatoes and pine nuts over the top.
■ Mix all the dressing ingredients together and season to taste. Drizzle over the salad leaves – serve any leftover dressing in a jug on the side.
■ To make the croûtons, toast both sides of the bread. Rub the clove of garlic over the surfaces and then cut into little cubes. Scatter over the salad just before serving.

Serves 4

PER SERVING
■
89 kcals (372 kj)
Protein 4 g
Fat 3 g
Carbohydrate 11 g
Fibre 1 g

THAI TOFU DIP

VEGAN

If you are buying a ready-made curry paste, make sure it is vegetarian as some contain fish sauce. If you prefer to make your own, use the recipe below.

100 g/4 oz silken tofu
1 teaspoon vegetable oil
1 small onion, finely chopped
1 tablespoon Thai green curry paste
2 tablespoons water

Green curry paste:
1 shallot, finely chopped
1 stalk lemon grass, chopped
2 small red chillies, chopped
2 garlic cloves, crushed
2.5-cm/1-in piece fresh root ginger, peeled and grated
grated zest of 1 lime
1 tablespoon chopped fresh coriander leaves and stalks

■ If making your own curry paste, grind all the ingredients in a pestle and mortar until you have a paste. (This will make more than you need. Store the excess in a screwtop jar in the refrigerator for up to 2 weeks.)
■ Drain the tofu and place in a blender or food processor.
■ Heat the oil and sauté the onion for 3 minutes. Add 1 tablespoon green curry paste and cook, stirring, for 2 minutes. Remove from the heat and cool.
■ Add to the tofu in the blender or food processor. Blend until smooth. Serve with a selection of raw vegetable crudités.

Serves 4

SUN-DRIED
TOMATO DIP

8 pieces of sun-dried tomato
1 garlic clove, crushed
grated zest and juice of 1 lemon
400-g/14-oz can of haricot beans,
    rinsed and drained

150 g/5 oz silken tofu
dash of Tabasco
salt and pepper
vegetable crudités, to serve

■ Soak the sun-dried tomatoes in boiling water to reconstitute. Drain, reserving the liquid.

■ Chop the tomatoes and place in a blender or food processor with the garlic, lemon zest and juice, beans and tofu. Blend to a dipping consistency, adding a little of the soaking water if required.

■ Season with Tabasco and salt and pepper to taste and serve with vegetable crudités.

Serves 6

PER SERVING
■
145 kcals (601 kj)
Protein 7 g
Fat 8 g
Carbohydrate 13 g
Fibre 4 g

TERIYAKI DRESSING

Teriyaki sauce is a ready-made marinade mixture, including shoyu, ginger, garlic, and honey among its ingredients. It makes an excellent basis for a salad dressing as well as for marinades.

2 tablespoons teryaki sauce
1 tablespoon rice vinegar
1 teaspoon sesame oil
1 teaspoon honey
1 tablespoon chopped fresh coriander
salt and pepper

■ Mix all the ingredients together and serve with a beansprout salad or a salad of exotic mushrooms. (It can also be used to marinate vegetables before grilling or cooking over hot coals on a barbecue.)

Serves 4

PER SERVING
■
28 kcals (117 kj)
Protein 0.6 g
Fat 1 g
Carbohydrate 4 g
Added sugar 3 g

SWEETCORN SALSA

PER SERVING
■
42 kcals (180 kj)
Protein 1 g
Fat 0.5 g
Carbohydrates 9 g
Added sugar 2 g
Fibre 1 g

A salsa is a cross between a dressing, a sauce and a salad – more of a relish. Wonderful served with salads, spicy foods and 'burgers', this recipe is very low in fat.

100 g/4 oz canned or frozen
   sweetcorn
25 g/1 oz onion, chopped
100 g/4 oz tomatoes, skinned and
   chopped
¼ cucumber, chopped
50 g/2 oz radish, sliced

1 red chilli, deseeded and finely
   chopped
15 g/½ oz fresh coriander or basil,
   chopped
juice of 1 lime
salt

■ If using frozen sweetcorn, cook according to the packet instructions and then cool.
■ Mix all the ingredients together and add a little salt to taste.
■ Leave the salsa to stand at room temperature, covered, for 1 hour before serving.

Serves 4

CUCUMBER, APPLE, ONION AND MINT RELISH

PER SERVING
■
32 kcals (137 kj)
Protein 1 g
Fat 0.1 g
Carbohydrate 7 g
Fibre 1 g

This relish is a good accompaniment for curries, cheese and salads and is very low in fat.

½ cucumber
2 dessert apples
1 small onion, chopped

1 tablespoon chopped mint
pinch of salt
1 tablespoon white wine vinegar

■ Cut the cucumber into quarters lengthways. Cut each long piece into 5-mm/¼-in chunks. Core the apples and cut into small cubes.
■ Mix all the ingredients together in a bowl and serve.

Serves 4

Opposite: Sweetcorn salsa and Cucumber, apple, onion and mint relish

VEGAN

BANANA, ONION
AND TOMATO CHUTNEY

This is a fresh chutney rather than a chutney for storing. Make just before serving as the banana can discolour and soften quickly.

PER SERVING
■
36 kcals (150 kj)
Protein 1 g
Fat 0.3 g
Carbohydrate 8 g
Fibre 1 g

1 banana, chopped
225 g/8 oz tomatoes, skinned and chopped
¼ red onion, finely chopped

15 g/½ oz fresh coriander chopped
juice of ½ lemon
salt
fresh coriander leaves, to garnish

■ Mix all the ingredients together in a bowl.
■ Garnish with coriander leaves and serve with Vegetable and Black Eye Bean Bangalore (see page 70) or Enchilladas with black bean and sweetcorn filling (see page 75) or other spicy dish of your choice.

Serves 4

VEGAN

FRESH ORANGE
AND DATE CHUTNEY

This is one of my favourite chutneys. We use it on the Cordon Vert diploma course as part of an Indian banquet.

PER SERVING
■
134 kcals (569 kj)
Protein 2 g
Fat 0.4 g
Carbohydrate 32.5 g
Fibre 2 g

225 g/8 oz stoned dates, coarsely chopped
2 oranges, peeled and segmented
juice of ½ lemon
3 tablespoons cider vinegar
120 ml/4 fl oz water
1 tablespoon maple syrup

2.5-cm/1-in piece fresh ginger root, peeled and thinly sliced
1 teaspoon yellow mustard seeds
1 teaspoon ground allspice or cinnamon
pinch of cayenne pepper
pinch of salt

■ Put all the ingredients into a saucepan and cook together over a low heat for about 45 minutes until soft. Cool.
■ Pour into a sterilized jar and seal. This chutney will keep for several weeks if refrigerated in a sealed container.

Serves 6

COURGETTE RELISH

VEGAN

I use up the glut of courgettes from the garden each year making this relish. It will keep in an airtight container in the refrigerator for up to three days.

1 tablespoon olive oil
225 g/8 oz courgettes, diced
1 small onion, chopped
¼ red pepper, very finely sliced
1 red chilli, very finely chopped

1 teaspoon yellow mustard seeds
3 tablespoons red wine vinegar
2 teaspoons light muscovado sugar
pinch of mustard powder
salt

■ Heat the oil and gently cook the courgettes, onion, red pepper, chilli and mustard seeds for 5 minutes.
■ Add the vinegar, sugar and mustard powder, mix well and continue to cook, stirring, for a further 5–10 minutes until the vegetables are tender and most of the liquid has evaporated. Season to taste.
■ Cool, chill in the refrigerator and serve with Mushroom, Pepper and Tomato Stew (see page 71).

Serves 4

PER SERVING
■
58 kcals (240 kj)
Protein 2 g
Fat 3 g
Carbohydrate 5.5 g
Fibre 1 g

ONION MARMALADE

VEGAN

This 'marmalade' can be used as a relish to serve with dishes such as Wild Mushroom Risotto (see page 68) or Bubble and Squeak Patties (see page 62). It is also delicious scattered over a simple green salad with a squeeze of lemon juice.

1 tablespoon olive oil
2 red onions, sliced
1 tablespoon light muscovado sugar

150 ml/¼ pint wine
salt and pepper

■ Heat the oil in a frying pan and sweat the onions over a low heat until starting to brown. Add the sugar, cover and cook gently for about 10 minutes until caramelized.
■ Remove the lid, add the wine and cook until the liquid has almost disappeared. Season to taste and serve as a relish with savoury dishes.

Serves 4

PER SERVING
■
78 kcals (325 kj)
Protein 0.4 g
Fat 3 g
Carbohydrates 7.5 g
Fibre 0.4 g

DESSERTS

Strawberries with black pepper
Lemon grass sorbet
Plum and cherry summer pudding
Peach and pear compote with cinnamon
Strawberry mousse
Mango and orange fool
Orange, almond and cinnamon biscuits
Tofu cheesecake
Brandied apricot stacks
Apple and blackberry filo pie
Fruity topping
Rice pudding
Apple and date cake
Stuffed pears with ginger custard
Apple, orange and raspberry nutty crumble

Left: Brandied apricot stacks (page 118)

STRAWBERRIES
WITH BLACK PEPPER

This rather unlikely combination is very refreshing served with the Lemon Grass Sorbet below.

450 g/1 lb ripe English strawberries
1 tablespoon balsamic vinegar
1 teaspoon freshly ground black pepper

mint leaves and black pepper, to serve

■ Wash and halve the strawberries and place in a ceramic dish. Sprinkle over the balsamic vinegar and black pepper and toss gently.
■ Cover with clingfilm and leave to marinate for at least 30–60 minutes.
■ Serve decorated with mint leaves and a sprinkling of black pepper.

Serves 4

PER SERVING
■
34 kcals (141 kj)
Protein 1 g
Fat 0.1 g
Carbohydrate 7.5 g
Fibre 1 g

LEMON GRASS SORBET

This has the most refreshing, light flavour of any sorbet, perfect at the end of a richly flavoured meal.

175 g/6 oz caster sugar
300 ml/½ pint water

4 stalks lemon grass, cut into 2.5-cm/1-in lengths
juice of 3 lemons

■ Dissolve the sugar in the water in a saucepan over a low heat, stirring until thoroughly dissolved. Bruise the lemon grass with a rolling pin and add to the saucepan. Boil for 3–4 minutes to make a sugar syrup.
■ Remove from the heat and leave to infuse for 1 hour. Strain through a fine sieve and stir in the lemon juice. Pour into a polythene container and freeze, uncovered, until half-frozen. Mash the mixture well and freeze until solid.
■ Remove the sorbet from the freezer 10–20 minutes before serving. Mash with a fork to break up the ice crystals, then shape between 2 serving spoons.

Serves 6

**PER SERVING
(EXCLUDING LEMON GRASS)**
■
116 kcals (493 kj)
Carbohydrate 31 g
Added sugar 31 g

PEAR SORBET VARIATION
■
Peel, core and stew 675 g/ 1½ lb pears. Purée the pears; boil the stewing liquid until reduced to 300 ml/½ pint. Mix together and freeze as for the Lemon Grass Sorbet.

Opposite: Lemon grass sorbet with Strawberries with black pepper

VEGAN

PLUM AND CHERRY
SUMMER PUDDING

This is an autumnal variation on an old favourite which is usually made with summer berries. If you can't get fresh fruit, use canned fruit in natural juice; if the fruit is in syrup, reduce the amount of caster sugar added.

450 g/1 lb plums, stoned
450 g/1 lb cherries, stoned
100 g/4 oz caster sugar
10 slices white bread, crusts removed
cherry pairs on stalks, to decorate

■ Place the fruit in a saucepan with the sugar and 2 tablespoons water. Cover and cook over a gentle heat until soft. Cool and drain, reserving the juice.
■ Cut out a circle of bread to fit the base of a 900-ml/1½-pint pudding basin. Cut the remaining bread into 2.5-cm/1-in wide strips.
■ Dip the bread into the reserved juice and use to line the pudding basin, overlapping the strips.
■ Spoon the fruit into the lined basin and add any remaining juice. Cover with the remaining bread.
■ Place a small plate on top of the bread. Put a weight on top and refrigerate overnight.
■ Turn out the summer pudding onto a serving plate and decorate with pairs of cherries.

Serves 6

PER SERVING
■
188 kcals (791 kj)
Protein 3 g
Fat 0.5 g
Carbohydrate 45 g
Fibre 2 g

PEACH AND PEAR
COMPOTE WITH CINNAMON

VEGAN

100 g/4 oz dried pears
100 g/4 oz dried peaches
5-cm/2-in piece of cinnamon stick
150 ml/¼ pint red wine

150 ml/¼ pint water
1 apple and cinnamon tea bag
(optional)

PER SERVING
■
137 kcals (573 kj)
Protein 1 g
Fat 0.4 g
Carbohydrates 27.5 g
Fibre 4 g

■ Place the dried pears and peaches in a saucepan with the cinnamon stick. Mix the wine and water together and pour over the dried fruit. Add the tea bag, if using, and leave to soak for 1–2 hours.

■ Place the pan over a gentle heat and cook the fruit for about 30 minutes until soft.

■ Serve hot or cold with Pear Sorbet (see page 110).

Serves 4

STRAWBERRY MOUSSE

VEGAN

If you use English strawberries in season, you should not need to add any sugar to this colourful dessert. Children will love it.

225 g/8 oz silken tofu
450 g/1 lb ripe strawberries, washed
and dried
grated zest of 1 orange

2 tablespoons crème de cassis
(optional)
15 g/½ oz icing sugar (optional)

PER SERVING
■
70 kcals (292 kj)
Protein 5 g
Fat 2.5 g
Carbohydrate 7 g
Fibre 1 g

■ Drain the tofu and place in a blender or food processor.

■ Reserve 4 strawberries with the calyx intact. Roughly chop the rest and add to the blender or food processor with the orange zest and crème de cassis (if using).

■ Blend well until smooth, and then spoon into sundae glasses and chill in the refrigerator.

■ Slice through the reserved strawberries upwards from the base, leaving the top and calyx intact, and fan them out. Decorate each chilled mousse with a fanned strawberry and serve with Orange, Almond and Cinnamon Biscuits (see page 116).

Serves 4

MANGO AND
ORANGE FOOL

To reduce the fat content in this dessert you could leave out the soya cream from the recipe, but for a special treat, the extra creaminess is welcome.

PER SERVING
■
201 kcals (836 kj)
Protein 7 g
Fat 11 g
Carbohydrate 19 g
Fibre 3.5 g

225 g/8 oz silken tofu
150 ml/¼ pint soya cream
5-cm/2-in piece fresh root ginger, peeled and grated
2 ripe mangoes
1 orange
2 tablespoons caster sugar
1 teaspoon vanilla essence

■ Drain the tofu and place in a blender with the soya cream and grated ginger. Peel and stone 1 mango and roughly chop the flesh. Add to the blender.
■ Zest the orange and reserve some of the strips for decoration. Put the remaining zest in the blender with the sugar and vanilla essence. Blend until smooth.
■ Peel, stone and cube the remaining mango. Segment the orange and chop each segment into 3. Mix together.
■ Divide half of the tofu mixture between 4 sundae glasses. Layer the fruit on top and cover with the remaining tofu mixture. Chill in the refrigerator.
■ Decorate with the reserved orange zest and serve with Orange, Almond and Cinnamon Biscuits (see page 116).

Serves 4

Opposite: Mango and orange fool with
Orange, almond and cinnamon biscuits (page 116)

ORANGE, ALMOND
AND CINNAMON BISCUITS

PER SERVING

■

132 kcals (550 kj)
Protein 2 g
Fat 9 g
Carbohydrate 11 g
Fibre 1 g

Although these biscuits contain quite a lot of fat, they are delicious served with a low-fat dessert such as Strawberry Mousse (see page 113) to add a little 'crunch'.

50 g/2 oz self-raising flour
50 g/2 oz ground almonds
25 g/1 oz porridge oats
25 g/1 oz demerara sugar
1 teaspoon ground cinnamon
grated zest and juice of 1 orange
50 g/2 oz soft vegan margarine
1 teaspoon orange essence

■ Preheat the oven to 180°C/350°F/Gas Mark 4.

■ Mix the flour, ground almonds and porridge oats together in a large bowl. Add the sugar, cinnamon and orange zest and mix well.

■ Melt the margarine in a saucepan together with the orange juice. Stir into the dry ingredients together with the orange essence. Mix to form a smooth dough, adding a little more orange juice if necessary.

■ Turn out onto a lightly floured surface and roll out to about 5 mm/¼ in thick. Use a 5-cm/2-in pastry cutter to make 12 biscuits. Place on a greased baking sheet and bake in the preheated oven for 20–30 minutes.

■ Cool on a wire rack and serve with the dessert of your choice.

Makes 8 biscuits

TOFU CHEESECAKE

Tofu makes an excellent substitute for cream cheese in this dessert, reducing the fat level considerably.

175 g/6 oz vegan ginger biscuits
50 g/2 oz vegan margarine

Topping:
300 g/10 oz silken tofu, drained
1 tablespoon maple syrup
225 g/8 oz raspberries (defrost if using frozen)
3 tablespoons agar agar flakes
150 ml/¼ pint water

To decorate:
15 g/½ oz toasted desiccated coconut
extra raspberries and sprigs of mint

PER SERVING
■
194 kcals (810 kj)
Protein 4 g
Fat 12 g
Carbohydrates 18 g
Added sugar 1 g
Fibre 3 g

■ Crush the ginger biscuits with a rolling pin to make fine crumbs.
■ Melt the margarine in a saucepan and stir in the crumbs. Press immediately into a 17-cm/7-in spring-mould tin. Chill in the refrigerator.
■ Put the silken tofu and maple syrup in a blender or food processor.
■ Push the raspberries through a plastic sieve to remove the pips and add the pulp to the blender or food processor. Blend until smooth.
■ Place the agar agar and water in a small saucepan. Bring to the boil, stirring all the time, then reduce the heat and simmer until dissolved. Add to the blender or processor and blend again.
■ Pour over the chilled crumb base and leave to set in the refrigerator for at least 2 hours.
■ Turn out the cheesecake onto a serving plate. Sprinkle the toasted coconut round the top edge and decorate with raspberries and sprigs of mint.

Serves 8

BRANDIED
APRICOT STACKS

PER SERVING
■
260 kcals (1085 kj)
Protein 7 g
Fat 7 g
Carbohydrates 45 g
Added sugar 0.6 g
Fibre 2 g

An elegant dish for a dinner party, this dessert uses filo pastry which has a lower fat content than puff or shortcrust pastry.

100 g/4 oz filo pastry
15 g/½ oz vegan margarine, melted
100 g/4 oz dried apricots, finely chopped
2 tablespoons brandy
600 ml/1 pint cold thick custard (made with soya milk)

To decorate:
icing sugar, for dusting
sprigs of mint

■ Preheat the oven to 200°C/400°F/Gas Mark 6.
■ Take 3 sheets of filo pastry at a time, and brush each layer with a little melted margarine. Lay the sheets on top of each other. Use a pastry cutter to cut into 7.5-cm/3-in disks. You will need 12 altogether.
■ Brush the top of each disk with a little melted margarine and place on a baking sheet lined with baking parchment. Cover with another sheet of baking parchment and another baking sheet. Place an ovenproof dish on top to weigh it down and bake in the preheated oven for 10–15 minutes until cooked. Cool.
■ Soak the apricots in brandy for 30 minutes, and then stir into the cold custard.
■ Place one disk of filo on each of 4 serving plates. Spoon the apricot custard on top. Repeat with another layer of each and top with a filo disk. Sift a little icing sugar over the stack, decorate with mint sprigs and serve.

Serves 6

Note: You may want to make a few extra disks of filo pastry to allow for breakages as they are quite fragile.

Opposite: Brandied apricot stacks

APPLE AND
BLACKBERRY FILO PIE

Blackberries are a good source of vitamin C. If you are picking your own, choose a site well away from the roadside.

450 g/1 lb cooking apples, peeled, cored and sliced
225 g/8 oz blackberries, washed
50 g/2 oz sugar

1 teaspoon mixed spice (optional)
3 sheets filo pastry
15 g/½ oz vegan margarine, melted
25 /1 oz flaked almonds

■ Preheat the oven to 190°C/375°F/Gas Mark 5.
■ Stew the apples gently in a little water for about 10 minutes until nearly cooked.
■ Allow to cool, then layer the apples and blackberries in a pie dish and sprinkle over the sugar and mixed spice (if using).
■ Brush one sheet of filo with melted margarine and place over the filling. Trim to fit. Repeat with the remaining 2 sheets.
■ Sprinkle the flaked almonds over the top and bake in the preheated oven for 20–30 minutes until golden.

Serves 4

FRUITY TOPPING

Serve this delicious low-fat topping with desserts in place of cream or soya cream.

225 g/8 oz silken tofu, drained
juice and grated zest of 1 orange
½ teaspoon orange essence

1 teaspoon lemon juice
1 tablespoon Cointreau (optional)

■ Blend all the ingredients together in a blender. Cover and chill in the refrigerator until needed.
■ Use as a vegan substitute for cream on fruity desserts.

Serves 8

Opposite: Apple and blackberry filo pie

RICE PUDDING

This traditional pudding is high in carbohydrate and vitamins. You can vary the fresh fruit according to what is in season.

50 g/2 oz flaked rice
600 ml/1 pint skimmed milk or soya milk*
25 g/1 oz raw sugar
50 g/2 oz sultanas

½ teaspoon ground nutmeg or cinnamon
1 apple, cored and sliced
1 orange, peeled and segmented
1 peach, stoned and sliced

∎ Place the flaked rice, milk, sugar, sultanas and spices in a saucepan. Bring to the boil, then reduce the heat and gently simmer, covered, for about 15 minutes until the rice is soft. Stir frequently to prevent sticking.
∎ Spoon the rice pudding into a serving dish and decorate with the fresh fruit. Serve immediately.

Serves 6

APPLE AND DATE CAKE

There is no added sugar in this cake. The sweetness comes from the fruit itself.

225 g/8 oz self-raising flour
1 teaspoon ground cinnamon
1 tablespoon lemon juice
150 ml/5 fl oz low-fat natural yogurt
2 free-range eggs, beaten

100 ml/4 fl oz vegetable oil
225 g/8 oz Bramley apples, peeled, cored and diced
100 g/4 oz chopped dates

∎ Preheat the oven to 180°C/350°F/Gas Mark 4. Grease and line a deep 20-cm/8-in cake tin with baking parchment.
∎ Sift the flour and cinnamon into a large mixing bowl. Beat the lemon juice, yogurt, eggs and oil together and add to the flour. Beat well to combine. Stir in the apples and dates and spoon into the prepared cake tin.
∎ Bake in the preheated oven for about 1¼ hours until risen and golden brown. Allow to cool for 5 minutes in the tin and then turn out onto a wire cooling rack.
∎ Serve cold with low-fat fromage frais or soya cream, if liked.

Serves 8

STUFFED PEARS
WITH GINGER CUSTARD

A wintry combination of pears, ginger and custard makes this dessert, which is high in carbohydrate, very more-ish! It has a tantalisingly festive smell, reminiscent of Christmas, when cooking.

4 large pears, peeled and cored

50 g/2 oz dried mixed fruit

1 piece stem ginger in syrup, finely chopped

2 tablespoons syrup from the ginger

4 tablespoons vegan custard powder*

25 g/1 oz caster sugar

1 teaspoon ground ginger

600 ml/1 pint skimmed milk or soya milk*

- Preheat the oven to 190°C/375°F/Gas Mark 5.
- Place the pears in an ovenproof dish.
- Mix the dried fruit, ginger and syrup together and use to fill the cavities in the pears. Put 4 tablespoons water in the dish, cover with foil and bake in the preheated oven for 40–45 minutes until tender.
- Mix the custard powder*, sugar and ground ginger together with a little of the milk. Heat the remaining milk in a saucepan. Pour over the custard powder, mix well then return to the pan and simmer for 3 minutes, stirring all the time, until thick. Serve with the stuffed pears.

Serves 4

PER SERVING
■

228 kcals (962 kj)

Protein 6 g

Fat 0.5 g

Carbohydrate 53 g

Fibre 3 g

VEGAN

APPLE, ORANGE
AND RASPBERRY NUTTY CRUMBLE

PER SERVING
■
269 kcals (1120 kj)
Protein 6 g
Fat 17 g
Carbohydrate 25 g
Fibre 4 g

It is difficult to make a dish involving nuts low in fat! This recipe relies on almonds and muesli to give the crunch to the crumble topping and these ingredients are good source of protein for vegetarians, so sometimes one has to be weighed against the other.

100 g/4 oz ground almonds
50 g/2 oz muesli
50 g/2 oz vegan margarine
25 g/1 oz demerara sugar
soya cream or ice cream, to serve

Fruit filling:
225 g/8 oz cooking apples, peeled, cored and sliced
2 oranges, peeled and all pith removed
225 g/8 oz raspberries (frozen)
25 g/1 oz caster sugar

■ Preheat the oven to 180°C/350°F/Gas Mark 4.
■ To make the nutty topping, mix the ground almonds and muesli together in a bowl. Rub in the vegan margarine and stir in the sugar.
■ Layer the apples in an ovenproof dish. Cut the oranges across the grain to make circles and place on top of the apples. Top with the raspberries and sprinkle over the sugar.
■ Spoon the nutty topping evenly over the fruit and bake in the preheated oven for 40–50 minutes. Serve hot with soya cream or ice cream.

Serves 6

Opposite: Apple, orange and raspberry nutty crumble

SNACKS,
SANDWICHES
AND DRINKS

Chilli tamari seeds
Smoked tofu and tomatoes on grilled ciabatta
Cheesy mushroom scramble on toasted
  baguette
Filled bagels
Pitta pockets with hummus and sprouted
  beans
Pitta pockets with rocket and tabbouleh salad
Pitta pockets with falafels
Tortilla wrap with bean and salsa filling
Bruschetta
Jacket potatoes with healthy toppings
Strawberry smoothie drink
Tropical drink

Left: Tortilla wrap with bean and salsa filling (page 134)

VEGAN

CHILLI TAMARI SEEDS

Serve these nutritious nibbles with drinks before a meal. Pumpkin seeds are an excellent source of zinc.

25 g/1 oz pumpkin seeds
25 g/1 oz sunflower seeds

½–1 teaspoon chilli powder
1–2 tablespoons tamari

- Place the seeds in a heavy-based pan without any oil. Toast over a high flame, shaking the pan to ensure that the seeds are evenly toasted. (You may want to put a lid on the pan as the seeds tend to crack and jump.)
- When the seeds are golden, remove from the heat and add the chilli powder. Shake or stir to coat.
- When the pan has cooled a little, add the tamari and stir well to coat.
- Serve as a nibble with drinks or use to scatter over plain green salads.

Serves 6

PER SERVING
■
53 kcals (221 kj)
Protein 2 g
Fat 4 g
Carbohydrate 2 g
Fibre 0.5 g

VEGAN

SMOKED TOFU
AND TOMATOES ON GRILLED CIABATTA

8 slices day-old ciabatta bread
225 g/8 oz packet smoked tofu
400-g/14-oz can of chopped tomatoes, drained

25 g/1 oz stoned olives
15 g/½ oz parsley, chopped
freshly ground black pepper

- Preheat the grill. Toast the ciabatta bread slices on both sides and keep warm.
- Slice the tofu into 'rashers' and grill gently on both sides for a couple of minutes until starting to colour. Cool a little and roughly chop.
- Place the drained tomatoes in a saucepan and heat through gently.
- Rinse the olives and drain well. Chop and add to the tomatoes together with the chopped tofu. Stir well to mix and heat through.
- Pile on top of the warm toast. Sprinkle with chopped parsley and coarsely ground black pepper. Serve immediately.

Serves 4

PER SERVING
■
214 kcals (907 kj)
Protein 14 g
Fat 6 g
Carbohydrate 32 g
Fibre 1 g

CHEESY MUSHROOM
SCRAMBLE ON
TOASTED BAGUETTE

This high protein, energy giving snack is a wonderful lunchtime treat on a cold winter's day.

1 small baguette or ½ French stick
4 tomatoes, halved
30 ml/2 fl oz skimmed milk
50 g/2 oz low-fat vegetarian
    Cheddar cheese, grated
6 free-range eggs, lightly beaten
salt and freshly ground black pepper
15 g/½ oz butter
50 g/2 oz button mushrooms, sliced
snipped chives, to garnish

■ Preheat the grill. Cut the baguette in half, then cut each piece in half along its length (as though making a sandwich). You should now have 4 long pieces of bread.

■ Toast under the preheated grill until golden. At the same time, grill the tomatoes.

■ Add the skimmed milk and grated cheese to the eggs and beat with a fork to combine. Season with a little salt and pepper.

■ Heat the butter in a large non-stick saucepan. Sauté the mushrooms for about 5 minutes until tender.

■ Pour the egg and cheese mixture into the pan. Stir continuously with a wooden spoon over a low heat until the softly scrambled egg forms. Remove from the heat and continue stirring until it reaches the required consistency.

■ Place the toasted baguettes on serving plates. Top each piece with the cheesy mushroom scramble. Garnish with the grilled tomatoes and sprinkle with snipped chives. Serve immediately.

Serves 4

PER SERVING
■
325 kcals (1364 kj)
Protein 20 g
Fat 16 g
Carbohydrate 27 g
Fibre 1 g

FILLED BAGELS

SUN-DRIED TOMATO AND BASIL SPREAD

PER SERVING
■
145 kcals (613 kj)
Protein 6 g
Fat 3 g
Carbohydrate 25 g
Fibre 1 g

zest and juice of ½ lemon
3 tablespoons sun-dried tomato purée
1 tablespoon ground almonds
15 g/½ oz basil leaves
salt and freshly ground black pepper
4 bagels, split and toasted

■ Mix the lemon zest and juice with the tomato purée and ground almonds to form a thick paste.
■ Chop half of the basil and stir in. Season with salt and pepper to taste.
■ Spread on the toasted bagels and scatter the remaining basil leaves over the top.

Serves 4

QUARK AND AVOCADO TOPPING

PER SERVING
■
185 kcals (782 kj)
Protein 12.5 g
Fat 4 g
Carbohydrate 27 g
Fibre 2 g

200 g/7 oz quark
½ avocado, peeled, stoned and
    chopped
juice of ½ lemon
12 cherry tomatoes, quartered
15 g/½ oz fresh coriander or parsley,
    chopped
salt and freshly ground black pepper
4 bagels, split and toasted

■ Mix the quark with the chopped avocado, lemon juice, cherry tomatoes and herbs. Season with salt and pepper, and use to top the toasted bagel slices.

Serves 4

Opposite: Filled bagels with Sun-dried tomato and basil spread and Quark and avocado topping

PITTA POCKETS
WITH HUMMUS AND SPROUTED BEANS

PER SERVING

■

441 kcals (1864 kj)
Protein 18 g
Fat 11 g
Carbohydrate 73 g
Fibre 7 g

400-g/14-oz can chick peas, rinsed
  and drained
2–3 tablespoons water
2 tablespoons tahini
juice of 1 lemon

1 tablespoon olive oil
2 garlic cloves, crushed
salt and pepper
4 pitta breads
100 g/4 oz mixed sprouted beans

■ Place the chick peas, water, tahini, lemon juice, olive oil and garlic in a food processor. Process until a rough pâté is achieved, adding more water if necessary. Season to taste.

■ Split the pitta breads down one side to make each into a pouch. Spread the hummus thickly inside and fill with sprouted beans.

Serves 4

PITTA POCKETS
WITH ROCKET AND TABBOULEH SALAD

PER SERVING

■

273 kcals (1162 kj)
Protein 9.5 g
Fat 2 g
Carbohydrate 57 g
Fibre 3 g

4 pitta breads
50 g/2 oz rocket leaves
50 g/2 oz endive
150 g/5 oz Mixed Grain Tabbouleh Salad (see page 86)
salad dressing of your choice

■ Split the pitta breads down one side to make each into a pouch.

■ Line each pitta bread with a mixture of rocket and endive leaves. Pile about 2 tablespoons of tabbouleh into each pocket and drizzle the salad dressing of your choice over.

Serves 4

PITTA POCKETS
WITH FALAFELS

VEGAN

400-g/14-oz can chick peas, rinsed and drained
75 g/3 oz onion, very finely diced
2 tablespoons finely chopped parsley
2 tablespoons finely chopped mint
2 garlic cloves, crushed
2 teaspoons ground coriander
2 teaspoons ground cumin
pinch of chilli powder
1 tablespoon gram flour mixed to a paste with 2 tablespoons water
salt and pepper
25 g/1 oz unbleached white flour
4 wholemeal pitta breads
50 g/2 oz mixed salad leaves

For the dressing:
150 ml/5 fl oz natural soya yogurt
1 tablespoon finely chopped mint
1 tablespoon lemon juice
salt to taste

PER SERVING
■
460 kcals (1953 kj)
Protein 21 g
Fat 7 g
Carbohydrate 84 g
Fibre 8 g

■ Preheat the oven to 190°C/375°F/Gas Mark 5. Lightly grease a baking sheet.
■ Grind the chick peas in a nut grinder or blender and transfer to a large bowl. Add the onion, parsley, mint, garlic and spices and mix well. Bind with the gram flour paste and season with salt and pepper.
■ Form the mixture into balls about the size of a walnut (it should make 12–16). Coat very lightly with unbleached flour, place on the greased baking sheet and cook in the preheated oven for about 20–25 minutes until golden, turning once.
■ Make the dressing by mixing the yogurt, mint and lemon juice together. Season to taste with salt.
■ Halve the pitta breads to make each into 2 small pockets. Chop the salad leaves roughly and fill each half. Push 2 falafels into each half and drizzle the dressing over. Serve immediately.

Serves 4

TORTILLA WRAP WITH
BEAN AND SALSA FILLING

Refried beans are pinto beans. If you can't buy them canned, use kidney beans and mash them lightly with a potato masher.

8 large soft flour tortillas
400-g/14-oz can of refried beans
1 quantity Tomato Salsa (see page 136)
4 spring onions, shredded

¼ cucumber, sliced
½ avocado, peeled, stoned and chopped
8 iceberg lettuce leaves, shredded

■ Preheat the oven to 190°C/375°F/Gas Mark 5.
■ Wrap the tortillas in foil and warm in the preheated oven for 5–10 minutes.
■ Meanwhile, place the refried beans in a bowl and add the salsa, spring onions, cucumber and avocado and mix well.
■ Place shredded lettuce on each tortilla. Top with the bean and salsa mixture. Fold each tortilla in half over the filling and roll up. Cut in half and serve.

Makes 8

BRUSCHETTA

Once fashionable, but now accepted as almost traditional on many menus, bruschetta make an excellent snack.

1 ciabatta loaf, cut into 12 slices
2 tablespoons vegan pesto
4 ripe tomatoes, skinned and roughly chopped

15 g/½ oz basil leaves, roughly torn
4 teaspoons balsamic vinegar
freshly ground black pepper

■ Preheat the grill and toast the ciabatta slices on both sides.
■ Spread a little vegan pesto on each slice. Top with tomato and basil leaves.
■ Drizzle the balsamic vinegar over the topping and grind some black pepper on top. Serve immediately.

Serves 4

Opposite: Tortilla wrap with bean and salsa filling

JACKET POTATOES
WITH HEALTHY TOPPINGS

PER AVERAGE
POTATO
■

245 kcals (1024 kj)
Protein 7 g
Fat 0.4 g
Carbohydrate 57 g
Fibre 5 g

4 large baking potatoes

Tahini and chive topping*:
juice of ½ lemon
3 tablespoons tahini
½ teaspoon yeast extract, dissolved
    in a little water
3 tablespoons water
15 g/½ oz chives, chopped
salt and pepper

**Low fat fromage frais
with herbs:**
200 g/7 oz low-fat fromage frais
handful of fresh herbs, e.g. basil and
    parsley, chopped
salt and pepper

Tomato salsa*:
225 g/8 oz ripe tomatoes, skinned
    and chopped
¼ red onion, finely chopped
15 g/½ oz fresh coriander, finely
    chopped
salt and pepper

Apple and hazelnut coleslaw*:
1 dessert apple, peeled and grated
50 g/2 oz cabbage, finely shredded
1 shallot, chopped
15 g/½ oz chopped roast hazelnuts
2 tablespoons Tofu Mayonnaise (see
    page 94) or ready-made vegan
    mayonnaise
1 teaspoon hazelnut oil

■ Cook the baking potatoes in a preheated oven at 200°C/400°F/Gas Mark 6,
for about 1–1½ hours until tender. Alternatively, cook in a microwave oven.
■ Mix all the ingredients of your chosen topping together thoroughly (use a
blender or food processor for the tahini and chive topping). Serve with jacket
potatoes.

Serves 4

Opposite: Jacket potatoes with healthy toppings

TAHINI TOPPING ■	FROMAGE FRAIS TOPPING ■	SALSA TOPPING ■	COLESLAW TOPPING ■
156 kcals (644 kj)	33 kcals (139 kj)	13 kcals (52 kj)	66 kcals (263 kj)
Protein 5 g	Protein 4 g	Protein 0.6 g	Protein 1 g
Fat 15 g	Fat 0.2 g	Fat 0.2 g	Fat 5 g
Carbohydrate 0.5 g	Carbohydrate 4 g	Carbohydrate 2 g	Carbohydrate 4 g
Fibre 2 g	Fibre 0.2 g	Fibre 0.6 g	Fibre 1 g

STRAWBERRY
SMOOTHIE DRINK

Strawberries are full of vitamin C and this is a very refreshing way of enjoying them. If you can buy English strawberries in season, you will find they are naturally sweeter than imported ones. If the drink is a little too tart for your taste, add a little icing sugar – but it won't be as healthy!

450 g/1 lb ripe strawberries, washed
1 banana
450 ml/15 fl oz low-fat natural
   yogurt

150 ml/¼ pint skimmed milk
1 teaspoon vanilla extract
6–8 ice cubes, crushed

■ Place the strawberries, banana, yogurt, milk and vanilla extract in a blender and blend until smooth.

■ Put the crushed ice into 4 tall glasses, pour the smoothie over the ice and serve immediately.

Serves 4

VEGAN

TROPICAL DRINK

600ml/1 pint pineapple juice, chilled
4 kiwi fruit, peeled and chopped
2 ripe mangoes, peeled, stoned and
   chopped

600 ml/1 pint soda water, chilled
6 ice cubes, crushed
sprigs of mint, to serve

■ Put the pineapple juice, kiwi fruit and mango flesh in a blender. Blend until smooth.

■ Pour into a large serving jug and chill in the refrigerator. Just before serving, add the soda water.

■ Place a little crushed ice in the bottom of each glass, pour over the drink and serve immediately.

Serves 6

Opposite: Tropical drink and Strawberry smoothie drink

MENU SUGGESTIONS

BREAKFASTS

Breakfast is the most important meal of the day. In literally breaking the fast that your body has been on while you have been sleeping, you boost your blood sugar and energy levels. Breakfasts tend to be high-carbohydrate meals in order to supply this energy, and it is a good rule to include a glass of orange juice or one or two pieces of fresh fruit to provide some of the vitamins that you need, especially vitamin C.

Here are some examples of balanced breakfasts that you can put together easily to give you a good start to the day:

MENU 1
- Fresh Fruit Salad with Granola and fromage frais or yogurt
- Savoury Muffin

High in carbohydrate and protein.

MENU 2
- Creamed Mushrooms on Toast, using the Seed or Herb Bread for toast
- Fruit Crêpes

High in carbohydrates, B vitamins, potassium and iron.

MENU 3
- Granola with milk or soya milk
- Cinnamon and Raisin Bread, toasted if liked, with a little butter or vegan margarine

This is reasonably high in fat because of the nuts in the granola and milk but it is a good protein meal, containing nuts, seeds, grains and milk/soya milk; the dried fruit is a good source of iron.

MENU 4
- Grilled Honeyed Citrus Fruits
- Baked Beans in Tomato Sauce
- Seed Bread, toasted

High in vitamin C and carbohydrates, and low in fat.

MENU 5
A weekend breakfast that could form brunch!
- Healthy Hash Browns with Tomatoes and Rashers, or Tofu Kedgeree
- Baked Beans in Tomato Sauce
- Breakfast Muffins and low-sugar preserves

This is a slightly larger breakfast for a late weekend start which could form both breakfast and lunch. Add an apple to give you a raw ingredient (remember, five-a-day) and this should carry you through the day until your evening meal.

LUNCHES

The sort of food you choose for lunch often depends on your lifestyle. If you are out at work all day and don't have access to cooking facilities at lunchtime, then one of the sandwich-style recipes may suit you. If you are at home all day, you may have more time for something like a soup which you can make in advance and then warm through quite quickly. Here are some suggestions for balanced lunches to suit different lifestyles:

MENU 1

Packed lunch for children, teenagers or adults.

Pick one of the following recipes and combine it with one or two pieces of fruit:
- Pitta Pockets with Hummus and Sprouted Beans
- Pitta Pockets with Falafels
- Pitta Pockets with Rocket and Tabbouleh Salad

These three recipes are high in protein and carbohydrates, and the sprouted beans and salads are full of vitamins, too. The rocket salad may be more suitable for an adult, being slightly bitter in flavour, but you could substitute other salad leaves for a child.

- Bagels with Quark and Avocado Topping

One of the few dairy recipes, but quark is very low in fat so this is still a healthy option. Fresh herbs and tomatoes supply a raw element as well as vitamins.

- Tortilla Wrap with Bean and Salsa Filling

An interesting lunch suited to teenagers and adults. Avocados are a good source of EFAs and B group vitamins and with the salad ingredients this lunch is full of vitamins as well as protein and carbohydrate.

MENU 2

Lunches for weekends or for people with access to cooking facilities at lunchtime.

- Jacket Potatoes with a variety of toppings

Potatoes are a good source of starchy carbohydrate and vitamin C. Combine a jacket potato with the topping of your choice. The tomato salsa and fromage frais with herbs toppings are particularly low in fat.

- Chickpea and Spinach Soup with Herb Bread

Chickpeas are high in protein and minerals and spinach is a good source of iron and vitamin C. This low fat soup will keep you going during the day.

- Pumpkin and Haricot Bean Soup with Seed Bread

A hearty soup for colder days, which is high in carbohydrate.

MENU 3

Light lunches.

- Minty Pea Dip with crudités

A light summery lunch, which is generally high in vitamins, particularly vitamin C. Team this with a low-fat fruit yogurt for dessert to increase the protein.

- Roast Pepper and Aubergine Mousse with Melba Toast

Red peppers are high in beta-carotene and make this dip an appetising colour.

- Fattoush with Lamb's Lettuce

This is reasonably high in fat because of the cheese and egg, but you could reduce this by using tofu instead or leaving this element out altogether. Lots of salad so again a good source of vitamins and a great way of contributing to your 5-a-day.

MAIN MEALS

In many households, the main meal is served in the evening as one or more family members are out of the home during the day, often taking a packed lunch with them. If you are able to eat your main meal at lunchtime and have a lighter evening meal or supper, this will give your body more chance to burn up the calories before you rest at night. Substitute the lunch suggestions above for a light evening snack or perhaps the Malaysian Vermicelli or Roast Vegetable Tortillas for something light but substantial.

For main meals the following combinations are suggested:

MENU 1

Quick weekday meals when you are probably too busy to spend a long time in the kitchen – a main course dish and vegetable/salad accompaniments followed by fresh fruit or yogurt is probably sufficient.

■ **Penne with Broccoli, Avocado and Roast Pepper**
Broccoli is sometimes called the ACE vegetable as it is high in vitamins A and C. The vitamin E in the avocado and pine nuts helps to protect these vitamins in the body.

■ **Asparagus Fettucine Stir-fry with Peanut Sauce, with Banana, Onion and Tomato Chutney**
Starchy pasta is a good source of carbohydrate and protein. The chutney provides vitamins, too, and the bananas are particularly high in potassium which helps to regulate the body's fluids. This meal is low in fat.

■ **Szechuan Tofu with rice and Japanese Sea Vegetable Salad**
A very tasty and quickly prepared mid-week meal. The rice, tofu and cashew nuts provide a good source of protein, but if you want to reduce the fat further either reduce the amount of cashew nuts or remove completely. The salad is very low in fat, and the sea

vegetables provide minerals and trace elements while the fresh vegetables are good for vitamins.

MENU 2

Low-calorie main meals

■ **Vegetable and Black Eye Bean Bangalore**
Although filling, this delicious curry is low in calories, but contains fresh fruit and vegetables to provide vitamins, and black eye beans for protein.

■ **Teryaki Stir-fry with Noodles and Sprouting Bean Salad with Ginger Dressing**
An oriental-style meal which is high in flavours but low in calories. The noodles provide protein while stir-frying the vegetables uses only a little fat and minimizes nutrient (vitamin) loss from the vegetables.

For low-calorie desserts try:
■ Strawberry Mousse
■ Lemon Grass Sorbet

MENU 3

Low-fat main meals.

■ **Farfalle with Mange Tout, Flageolet Beans, Courgettes and Mint**
You could serve this with a green salad dressed with lemon juice in place of the garlic bread, if liked, but it will also stand on its own and is both tasty and nutritious. The pasta and cheese provide protein and the vegetables are a good source of vitamins.

■ **Millet Pilaf with Spicy Bean Salad**
This is low in fat but good for protein and carbohydrate with a wide range of vegetables and pulses for vitamins, too. Quite a hearty meal, good for winter.

For low-fat desserts try:
■ Rice Pudding
■ Plum and Cherry Summer Pudding

MENU 4

Teenager's menu.

- Potato Pizza with Mixed Pepper and Mushroom Topping
- Strawberry Mousse

Obviously you can change the pizza topping, but the base is a good source of carbohydrate and protein while the topping with the range of vegetables is full of vitamins. The recipes provide a reasonable level of fat and of calories to provide fuel for active teenagers.

- Bubble and Squeak Patties served with steamed vegetables or Mixed Green Salad with Tofu and Mango
- Apple and Blackberry Filo Pie

These healthy oven-baked patties or burgers are great for a main meal. Teenagers need lots of calcium so introducing tofu, which often has a high-calcium but low-fat content, can be a good way of achieving this. The pie is filling, but not too high in calories, while providing fruit to increase vitamin intake.

MENU 5

High-protein menu.

One of the questions frequently asked is 'Will I get enough protein on a vegetarian diet?'. There really is no problem with this as you will see from the analysis of the recipes. However, if you need a high-protein diet for a particular reason try some of the following.

For high-protein starters or light meals:

- Pumpkin and Haricot Bean Soup
- Tuscan Tomato Soup
- Broad Bean, Lemon and Sage Dip
- Caponata Crostini

For high-protein main dishes:

- Farfalle with Mange Tout, Flageolet Beans, Courgettes and Mint
- Broad Bean and Sweetcorn Stew
- Marinated Tofu and Vegetable Filo Pie

Serve any of the above with steamed vegetables or salad of your choice for all-round balance.

For high protein desserts:

- Apple, Orange and Raspberry Nutty Crumble
- Stuffed Pears with Ginger Custard

MENU SUGGESTIONS FOR HEALTHY ENTERTAINING WITHOUT MISSING OUT!

For some reason it seems to be generally thought that if you are eating 'healthy' food or vegetarian food, you must be missing out on the treats. Combine the words 'healthy', 'vegetarian' and 'food' and most omnivores will think you wear a hair shirt, too! Prove to your guests that food that is good for you can be enjoyable and vice versa, with the following menu suggestions:

MENU 1

Far Eastern Evening:
- Chinese-style Lettuce Wraps
- Szechan Tofu with rice
- Rice Noodle Salad with Oriental Vegetables
- Lemon Grass Sorbet

MENU 2

A Summer Dinner Party:
- Roast Pepper and Aubergine Mousse with melba toasts
- Asparagus Fettucine Stir-fry with Peanut Sauce
- Wild Flower and Herb Salad
- Brandied Apricot Stacks

MENU 3

A Winter/Christmas menu:
- Carrot Soup
- Sweet and Sour Cabbage Parcels
- Celeriac Mash
- Steamed green vegetables of your choice (e.g. beans and broccoli)
- Peach and Pear Compote with Cinnamon

ENTERTAINING

Sharing good food with friends and family gives you a chance to be creative in the kitchen and this section of the book concentrates on recipe ideas for various situations where you may want to use your skills to produce exciting vegetarian food, from formal dinner parties to al fresco entertaining.

The recipes have all been tested in The Vegetarian Society's own Cordon Vert Cookery School and reflect the international range of cookery styles taught on the Cordon Vert courses. There are useful hints and tips for both beginner and the more experienced cook, and in some chapters full menus have been suggested with wine notes where appropriate. However, you can easily devise your own menus and you will find that most of the recipes are suitable for vegans or can be easily adapted.

The Cordon Vert Cookery School encourages anyone interested in cooking, from amateur to professional, to explore the exciting colours and flavours of vegetarian cuisine and to share the pleasure of wonderful food with friends old and new. So spoil your friends with gourmet vegetarian delights. Enjoy.

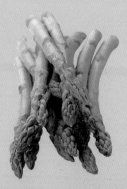

INFORMAL
SUPPERS

*Left: Exotic vegetable stir-fry (page 160) and Halloumi
and mango with a mint dressing (page 148)*

HALLOUMI AND MANGO
WITH A MINT DRESSING

Halloumi and mango are a really delicious combination. Cook the Halloumi just before serving; if allowed to go cold, it quickly becomes rubbery in texture.

250 g / 9 oz Halloumi cheese
6 tablespoons seasoned flour
200 g / 7 oz mixed salad leaves
1 ripe mango, peeled, stoned
  and sliced
8 g / ⅓ oz mint, finely chopped

150 ml / 5 fl oz natural yogurt
juice of ½ lemon
salt and freshly ground black pepper
3 tablespoons groundnut oil
100 g / 4 oz cherry tomatoes, halved
sprigs of mint, to garnish

■ Cut the Halloumi into 8 slices and then cut each in half. Coat in the seasoned flour and put aside. Arrange the salad leaves on 4 serving plates and place the slices of mango on top.

■ Make the dressing: mix the chopped mint, yogurt and lemon juice together in a bowl and season to taste.

■ Heat the oil in a non-stick frying pan or griddle and quickly fry the Halloumi for about 2 minutes on each side, until golden.

■ Drizzle the yogurt dressing over the salad leaves and mango. Arrange the fried Halloumi on top. Garnish with cherry tomatoes and mint sprigs and serve immediately with extra dressing on the side.

Serves 4 as a starter or 2 as a main course

HOT AND SOUR
SOUP

*CAN BE VEGAN

Chinese hot and sour soup usually involves shredded meat, but can easily be made vegetarian by using marinated tofu in its place. Adjust the shoyu, chilli and sesame oil to suit your own taste.

4 dried shiitake mushrooms

1.2 litres/2 pints vegetable stock

225 g/8 oz canned bamboo shoots, drained and shredded

225 g/8 oz marinated tofu, cut into thin strips

2 small red chillies, deseeded and finely chopped

3 tablespoons white wine vinegar

2 tablespoons shoyu

1 tablespoon cornflour

4 tablespoons water

1 free-range egg, beaten (omit for vegans*)

2 teaspoons toasted sesame oil

2 spring onions, shredded

■ Soak the dried mushrooms in hot water for about 15–20 minutes. Drain through fine muslin, reserving the liquid. Remove the stalks from the mushrooms and discard. Slice the mushrooms into thin strips.

■ Place the mushrooms in a saucepan with the stock and bring to the boil. Simmer for 10 minutes. Add the bamboo shoots, marinated tofu and chillies and simmer for a further 5 minutes. Add the vinegar and shoyu.

■ Mix the cornflour with the water until a paste is formed and add to the soup, stirring all the time until thickened.

■ Take the soup off the heat and stir in the beaten egg, if using. Season with the toasted sesame oil and garnish with spring onion shreds.

Serves 4

TIP

■

You can use fresh shiitake mushrooms in this soup if you prefer. Wipe the caps and remove and discard the stems before slicing and continue as before. Dried shiitake mushrooms can be purchased very cheaply in Chinese supermarkets where they are usually labelled as 'Dried Mushrooms'.

SUITABLE FOR VEGANS

SOUPE
AU PISTOU

A hearty, warming peasant soup — good to come home to after a wintry walk with friends or weekend guests. It can be prepared in advance and reheated when required.

TIP
■

In the summer when basil is plentiful and can be grown in your garden, make your own pesto. Put a handful of basil into a blender jug with one or two cloves of crushed garlic, 25 g/1 oz pine kernels, a pinch of salt, 1 tablespoon lemon juice and 4–6 tablespoons of olive oil. Blend well.

4 tablespoons olive oil
1 large onion, finely chopped
2 garlic cloves, crushed
2 sticks celery, finely chopped
225 g/8 oz carrots, finely diced
2 × 425-g/15-oz cans cannellini
    beans, drained and rinsed
900 ml/1½ pints vegetable stock
425-g/15-oz can chopped tomatoes

2 tablespoons tomato purée
3 tablespoons vegan pesto
salt and freshly ground black pepper

To serve:
50 g/2 oz vegetarian Parmesan
cheese, grated (omit for vegans)
crusty French bread
small bunch fresh basil

■ Heat the oil in a large, heavy-based saucepan. Fry the onion, garlic and celery for 5–10 minutes, until beginning to brown. Add the carrots and cook for a further 5 minutes.

■ Blend one can of cannellini beans with 300 ml/½ pint of vegetable stock. Stir in the whole beans, chopped tomatoes, tomato purée and remaining vegetable stock and bring to the boil. Reduce the heat and simmer for about 30 minutes, until all the vegetables are tender. Stir in the pesto, making sure it is evenly distributed. Season to taste.

■ Serve the soup hot, sprinkled with Parmesan cheese (omit for vegans) and garnished with basil, with warm, crusty French bread.

Serves 4

Opposite: Soupe au pistou

BAKED AVOCADOS
WITH STILTON

Strong blue Stilton cheese and creamy avocado are a classic combination. If Stilton is not to your taste, try a tasty Lancashire instead. These baked avocados are rich and filling as a main course for four people or would serve eight as a starter.

4 medium ripe avocados
1 tablespoon lemon juice
2 ripe plum tomatoes, skinned and chopped (or use canned)
100 g/4 oz vegetarian blue Stilton, crumbled
25 g/1 oz pine nuts, lightly toasted
few sprigs of basil leaves, torn
salt and freshly ground black pepper

Vinaigrette:
2 tablespoons extra virgin olive oil
1 tablespoon lemon juice
salt and freshly ground black pepper

To garnish:
250 g/9 oz packet mixed herb salad leaves
pine nuts
few basil leaves

■ Preheat the oven to 190°C/375°F/Gas Mark 5.
■ Halve the avocados, remove the stones and brush a little lemon juice over the cut surfaces to stop them discolouring.
■ Mix the chopped tomatoes, Stilton, pine nuts and basil together. Season with salt and pepper and fill each avocado half with the mixture.
■ Place in an ovenproof dish and bake in the preheated oven for 10–15 minutes.
■ Meanwhile, make the vinaigrette by mixing the olive oil and lemon juice together. Blend and season well with salt and pepper.
■ Serve immediately, surrounded by mixed herb salad leaves, drizzled with vinaigrette and garnished with pine nuts and basil leaves.

Serves 4

CHILLED MARINATED
MUSHROOMS

This recipe needs to be prepared in advance to give the flavours time to develop. It is good served as a starter with crusty bread, or you can make half the quantity and serve it as part of an antipasto platter or as one of a variety of salads.

2 red peppers
4 tablespoons olive oil
2 onions, chopped
2 garlic cloves, crushed
2.5-cm/1-in piece fresh ginger root, grated
2 tablespoons tomato purée
4 whole cloves
150 ml/¼ pint white wine
2 tablespoons soft brown sugar
900 g/2 lb button mushrooms
2–3 tablespoons shoyu
salt and freshly ground black pepper

■ Preheat the oven to 200°C/400°F/Gas Mark 6.
■ Put the red peppers on a baking sheet and cook in the preheated oven until the skins are blackening. Remove from the oven, place in a plastic bag and, when cool enough to handle, remove the skin and seeds, and slice thinly. Set aside and reserve the juices.
■ Heat the olive oil in a heavy-based saucepan. Fry the onions, garlic and ginger until colouring. Stir in the tomato purée, cloves, white wine and sugar. Bring to the boil, then reduce the heat and simmer for 15 minutes, until the sauce is thick. Add the mushrooms and cook for a further 5 minutes.
■ Take off the heat, season with shoyu and salt and pepper and add the red pepper strips and reserved juices. Cover and, when cold, chill. Serve cold with a rice salad or crusty bread to soak up the marinade.

Serves 4

TIP
■
To make fresh ginger easier to grate, pare off the thin peel and freeze the ginger root. Grate from frozen. Fresh ginger keeps well in the fridge (about six weeks) or if you pot some up and keep it on your window sill you can grow your own and dig it up when you need it.

DEEP-FRIED POTATO
SKINS WITH TANGY DIPS

A popular supper dish, the potatoes can be cooked in advance and deep-fried at the last minute. If you don't have time to prepare the dips (which can also be made in advance and chilled), there are plenty to choose from 'off the shelf' in the supermarket!

8 large baking potatoes
2 tablespoons olive oil
salt
groundnut oil, for deep-frying

Honey mustard dip:
2 tablespoons white wine vinegar
2 tablespoons whole-grain mustard
2 tablespoons runny honey or
   maple syrup*
8 tablespoons olive oil

salt and freshly ground black pepper

Tangy tomato dip:
225 g/8 oz ripe tomatoes, skinned,
   deseeded and finely chopped
2 spring onions, finely chopped
1/2 bunch fresh coriander, chopped
1 teaspoon tabasco sauce
1 teaspoon balsamic vinegar
salt and freshly ground black
   pepper

■ Preheat the oven to 200°C/400°F/Gas Mark 6.

■ Scrub the potatoes, prick the skins and then brush with olive oil and sprinkle with salt. Place on a baking sheet and bake for about 50–60 minutes in the preheated oven, until tender when pierced with a fork.

■ Meanwhile, make the dips. For the honey mustard dip, mix together the vinegar, mustard and honey or maple syrup, then whisk in the olive oil, a tablespoon at a time, until thick and creamy. Season to taste.

■ For the tangy tomato dip, mix all the ingredients together and season to taste with salt and pepper.

■ When the potatoes are cooked, cut them in half lengthways and use a teaspoon to scoop out most of the flesh, leaving a layer of potato about 1 cm/1/2 in thick attached to the skin. Cut in half lengthways again.

■ Heat the groundnut oil in a wok. (The oil is hot enough when a small cube of bread dropped in sinks to the bottom, then immediately rises to the top, sizzling.)

■ Deep fry the potato skins, a few at a time, for about 1–2 minutes, until golden and crisp. Drain on kitchen paper and keep warm. When they are all cooked, sprinkle with salt and serve with the dips.

Serves 4

ALTERNATIVE DIPS
■

Tasty tartare
Mix 100 ml/4 fl oz crème fraîche with the juice of 1 lime, 1 tablespoon each of finely chopped capers and finely chopped gherkins, 1 crushed garlic clove and a handful of freshly chopped basil. Season to taste.

Olive dip
Chop 2 tablespoons green olives very finely and mix with 3 tablespoons olive oil, 1 tablespoon lemon juice and a handful of freshly chopped coriander. Season to taste.

Spicy mayo dip
Mix together 6 tablespoons vegetarian or vegan mayonnaise, 1 tablespoon mango chutney and 1 teaspoon of medium curry powder.

INDIVIDUAL
ARTICHOKE TARTS

A melt-in-the-mouth, very simple pastry that requires no rolling is combined with summery vegetables in these delicious little tarts. The balsamic vinegar sprinkled over the hot vegetables on serving brings out the flavour.

100 g /4 oz plain white flour
50 g /2 oz semolina
50 g /2 oz ground almonds
pinch of salt
100 g /4 oz butter or vegan margarine*
1 tablespoon cold water
4 teaspoons balsamic vinegar
basil leaves, to garnish

Artichoke filling:
2 tablespoons olive oil

100 g /4 oz red onions, halved
   and sliced
1 garlic clove, crushed
425 g /15 oz can artichoke hearts,
   drained and halved
2 spring onions, finely chopped
12 kalamata olives, stoned and
   finely chopped
100 g /4 oz cherry tomatoes, halved
salt and freshly ground black
   pepper

TIP
■

Fresh coriander also complements the flavour of artichokes and olives and may be used in place of the basil. A pinch of cayenne in the pastry also adds a little 'kick'.

■ Preheat the oven to 220°C/425°F/Gas Mark 7.
■ Mix the flour, semolina, ground almonds and salt in a bowl. Melt the butter or vegan margarine* with the water in a small saucepan. Pour into the dry ingredients and mix thoroughly to make a dough. Divide the dough into 4 pieces. Mould into four 10-cm/4-in loose-bottomed flan tins. Chill in the refrigerator for 30 minutes.
■ To make the filling, heat the oil and gently fry the red onions and garlic. Take off the heat and stir in all the other ingredients. Season well.
■ Spoon the filling into the flan cases and bake in the preheated oven for about 20–25 minutes, until the pastry is cooked and the vegetables are starting to char.
■ Turn out onto individual plates and sprinkle the vegetables with a little balsamic vinegar. Garnish with the basil leaves and serve.

Serves 4

*CAN BE VEGAN

ROAST VEGETABLE
AND SMOKED TOFU PLAIT

TIP

◾

If you prefer, you could use marinated tofu in place of smoked, or, for a non-vegan version, you could leave out the tofu and top the vegetables with pieces of vegetarian Brie just before enclosing the filling in the pastry.

This is a lovely use of smoked tofu which is now readily available on the supermarket shelves. Smoked garlic is also easier to find and adds to the smoky flavour.

1 medium courgette, sliced
1 medium aubergine, cut into 1-cm/½-in cubes
1 red pepper, cut into 1-cm/½-in cubes
225 g/8 oz shallots, peeled and cut in half
8 smoked garlic cloves, peeled and left whole
225 g/8 oz smoked tofu, cut into small cubes
4 tablespoons olive oil
salt and freshly ground black pepper
2 tablespoons pine nuts
450 g/1 lb puff pastry, thawed if frozen
flour for rolling out
1 free-range egg, lightly beaten, or 1 tablespoon soya flour and
    2 tablespoons water*
sesame or poppy seeds, to decorate

◾ Preheat the oven to 200°C/400°F/Gas Mark 6.
◾ Arrange the vegetables on a baking tray together with the smoked tofu. Drizzle with olive oil and bake in the preheated oven until the vegetables are tender and starting to char slightly. Season and leave to cool.
◾ Gently toast the pine nuts under a hot grill until golden. Mix into the vegetables.
◾ Roll out the pastry, 225 g/8 oz at a time on a floured surface, to an oblong 20 x 32 cm/8 x 13 in) and place on a greased baking tray. Arrange half the vegetable filling down the centre of each piece. Cut strips 1 cm/½ in wide on either side of the filling, leaving 1 cm/½ in uncut on either side of the filling. Bring alternate strips over to enclose the filling, securing with egg wash or soya flour paste*.
◾ Brush the top of the pastry with egg wash or soya paste* and decorate with sesame or poppy seeds. Bake in the preheated oven for 20–25 minutes, until crisp, well risen and golden.

Serves 4

Opposite: Roast vegetable and smoked tofu plait

CHEESY AUBERGINE
FILO PIE

Rich, cheesy and filling, this unusual pie has a slightly smoky flavour because the aubergines are baked. Make sure you prick them thoroughly all over with a fork or they will burst in the oven.

2 aubergines
2 tablespoons olive oil
25 g/1 oz butter
25 g/1 oz plain white flour
300–450 ml/½–¾ pint milk
50 g/2 oz mozzarella cheese, cut into cubes
75 g/3 oz vegetarian Cheddar cheese, grated
1 free-range egg, beaten

salt and freshly ground black pepper
pinch of nutmeg
225 g/8 oz filo pastry
olive oil, for brushing

For the topping:
25 g/1 oz vegetarian Cheddar cheese, grated
3 tablespoons breadcrumbs

■ Preheat the oven to 180°C/350°F/Gas Mark 4.

■ Wash and dry the aubergines and prick them all over with a fork. Place on a baking sheet and cook in the preheated oven for about 1 hour, turning several times. When tender, scoop out the flesh into a sieve and press lightly to extract the bitter juices. Chop the flesh roughly.

■ Make a white sauce. Melt the butter in a saucepan, add the flour and cook gently for 2–3 minutes, stirring all the time, to make a roux. Take the saucepan off the heat and add half of the milk, a little at a time, stirring constantly. Return to the heat, bring to the boil and simmer to thicken — if too thick, add more milk. When the desired consistency is reached, remove from the heat and stir in the mozzarella and Cheddar cheeses, beaten egg and chopped aubergine flesh. Season to taste with salt, pepper and nutmeg.

■ Unroll the filo pastry and cut to fit a greased 18-cm/7-in square cake tin. Keeping the unused pastry covered until needed, brush one sheet with olive oil and place in the base of the tin. Repeat with two more oiled sheets. Put half the cheese and aubergine mixture on top of the pastry. Brush three more sheets of pastry and place on top. Cover with the rest of the cheese and aubergine mixture. Finish with three more sheets of oiled filo pastry.

■ Mix the Cheddar and breadcrumbs together for the topping, and sprinkle over the top. Bake for about 1 hour, or until golden and set. Serve hot or at room temperature with a fresh green salad.

Serves 4

SAVOURY PANCAKES
WITH ROAST VEGETABLE FILLING

The pancakes can be made in advance, then stacked with sheets of greaseproof paper in between and frozen until required.

1 courgette, cut into 1-cm/½-in cubes
1 aubergine, cut into 1-cm/½-in cubes
8 shallots or small onions, quartered
8 garlic cloves, peeled and left whole
1 head fennel, cut into 1-cm/½-in pieces
1 red or yellow pepper, cut into 1-cm/½-in cubes
salt and freshly ground black pepper
4 tablespoons olive oil
1 tablespoon chopped fresh parsley
chopped fresh parsley, to garnish

Savoury pancakes:
50 g/2 oz plain white flour
50 g/2 oz gram (chick pea) flour, sieved
300 ml/½ pint soya milk
1 teaspoon groundnut oil

Tomato sauce:
1 tablespoon olive oil
1 onion, finely chopped
1 garlic clove, crushed
425-g/15-oz can chopped tomatoes
1 tablespoon red wine vinegar
1 tablespoon soft brown sugar
salt and freshly ground black pepper

■ Preheat the oven to 200°C/400°F/Gas Mark 6.

■ Place the prepared vegetables in a roasting pan. Season with salt and pepper and toss in olive oil. Roast in the preheated oven for 30–40 minutes, until golden. Remove from the oven, cool and stir in the chopped parsley. Reduce the oven temperature to 180°C/350°F/Gas Mark 4.

■ Make the pancake batter. Blend the flours and soya milk together and leave to stand for 20 minutes.

■ Meanwhile, make the sauce. Heat the oil in a heavy-based saucepan, and fry the onion and garlic until soft. Add the tomatoes, vinegar, sugar and seasoning to taste. Remove from the heat and set aside.

■ Heat the groundnut oil for the pancakes in an 18-cm/7-in non-stick frying pan. When really hot, pour in enough batter to thinly coat the pan. Cook over a moderate heat until the underside of the pancake is brown, turn over and cook the other side. Make 8 pancakes in total.

■ Place one pancake in a large greased ovenproof dish. Put some of the roasted vegetable filling in the centre and roll up. Repeat with the remaining pancakes and pack neatly into the dish. Cover with tomato sauce and bake in the oven for 30 minutes, until heated through. Serve garnished with parsley.

Serves 4

TIP
■

The variations on savoury pancakes are endless. Try adding a pinch of cumin and coriander to the pancake batter and fill the pancakes with your favourite vegetarian curry, omitting the tomato sauce and covering with foil before baking; or for a wintery dish, try a mixture of roasted root vegetables, such as butternut squash, carrots, parsnips, sweet potato and shallots, in place of the 'Mediterranean' vegetables in this recipe.

Exotic vegetable
STIR-FRY

The secret of making a crisp and delicious stir-fry is to prepare all the ingredients before you start cooking, to keep the oil hot and to cook those vegetables that will take the longest first.

2 tablespoons groundnut oil
1 red onion, cut in half and sliced
1 garlic clove, crushed
100 g/4 oz fresh shiitake mushrooms, stalks removed and sliced
1 red chilli, deseeded and finely chopped
2 baby aubergines, quartered
5-cm/2-in piece mooli, cut into thin circles
50 g/2 oz baby carrots, halved lengthways
50 g/2 oz baby sweetcorn, halved
50 g/2 oz mange tout, topped, tailed and halved

50 g/2 oz green beans, cut into 2.5-cm/1-in pieces
100 g/4 oz baby spinach leaves, washed

Szechuan sauce:
1 teaspoon fresh ginger juice
1 tablespoon shoyu
1 tablespoon lime juice
1 teaspoon szechuan pepper, ground

To serve:
225 g/8 oz white long-grain rice, boiled
2 spring onions, shredded or tassled
few sprigs of fresh coriander

■ Heat the oil in a wok. When really hot, add the red onion and garlic and fry for 2 minutes. Add the shiitake mushrooms and chilli and cook for 3 minutes. Then add the baby aubergines and cook for 5 minutes, stirring and tossing the vegetables all the time.

■ Add the mooli, carrots and sweetcorn and cook for 3 minutes, then the mange tout and green beans and cook for a further 3 minutes. Finally, add the baby spinach leaves. Stir and cook until wilted.

■ Mix together the sauce ingredients and toss into the stir-fried vegetables. Serve on a bed of boiled rice, garnished with spring onions and coriander.

Serves 4

TIP
■

To make fresh ginger juice, peel a 5-cm/2-in piece of fresh root ginger, then grate it and squeeze the juice out of the grated flesh. To extract the maximum amount of juice, put the flesh into a garlic press and squeeze — the juice will come through the holes, leaving the fibrous flesh behind.

MARINATED SPICED
AUBERGINES

SUITABLE FOR VEGANS

Aubergines and tomatoes are a classic flavour combination and the spicy marinade complements the vegetables. This would also make a good dish cooked on your barbecue.

7 tablespoons olive oil

2 garlic cloves, crushed

1/2 teaspoon ground coriander

1/2 teaspoon ground cumin

1/4–1/2 teaspoon chilli powder

salt and freshly ground black pepper

2 medium aubergines, each sliced
  into four lengthways

1/2 teaspoon whole coriander seeds,
  lightly crushed

1/2 teaspoon whole cumin seeds,
  lightly crushed

1 onion, sliced

450 g/1 lb ripe tomatoes, skinned
  and sliced

crusty bread, to serve

■ Preheat the oven to 190°C/375°F/Gas Mark 5.

■ Mix 6 tablespoons of the olive oil with one of the crushed garlic cloves. Add the ground spices and season with salt and pepper.

■ Brush both sides of each aubergine slice with the seasoned oil. Lay the slices in a shallow dish, pour over any remaining marinade and cover. Leave to marinate for 30–60 minutes.

■ Heat the remaining olive oil in a saucepan and gently fry the coriander and cumin seeds for a few seconds. Add the onion and remaining garlic and cook until golden brown. Add the tomatoes and cook for 5 minutes. Season to taste with salt and pepper and then set aside.

■ Grill the marinated aubergines until cooked on both sides (or cook on a griddle pan to give the aubergines charred stripes). Place the grilled aubergines in a shallow ovenproof dish or roasting pan.

■ Reheat the tomato and onion mixture and spread over the aubergines. Heat through in the preheated oven for about 20 minutes. Serve hot with plenty of crusty bread.

Serves 4

TIP
■

At one time aubergines needed to be 'degorged' by sprinkling the cut surfaces with salt to draw out the bitter juices. Modern varieties are much less bitter and it is no longer necessary to do this. These aubergines could be served as part of an Indian meal with Naan Bread, or with a bulgar wheat salad. Just mix 225 g/8 oz soaked bulgar wheat with some finely chopped cucumber and 3 skinned and chopped tomatoes. Add a handful of chopped fresh herbs of your choice, mix with a classic vinaigrette and season well.

PASTA WITH LEEKS IN A
TARRAGON CREAM SAUCE

This pasta dish is extremely quick to make and ideal for an informal meal with friends. The sauce can be cooked at the same time as the pasta and the whole process takes less than 20 minutes.

225 g / 8 oz conchiglie (pasta shells)
25 g / 1 oz butter or vegan margarine*
225 g / 8 oz leeks, trimmed and finely shredded
1 garlic clove, crushed
12 g / 1/2 oz dried ceps (porcini), soaked in warm water for about 15 minutes
25 g / 1 oz plain white flour
150 ml / 1/4 pint vegetable stock
150 ml / 1/4 pint vegetarian white wine
2 tablespoons chopped fresh tarragon
salt and freshly ground black pepper
3 tablespoons single cream or soya cream*

■ Cook the pasta in boiling lightly salted water according to the manufacturer's instructions. Drain well.
■ Meanwhile, make the sauce. Melt the butter or vegan margarine* in a large, heavy saucepan. Gently cook the leeks and garlic until tender. Drain the ceps, chop very finely and add to the pan.
■ Stir in the flour. Take the pan off the heat and gradually add the stock and white wine, stirring all the time to prevent lumps from forming.
■ Put the pan back on the heat, bring to the boil, then simmer for 5 minutes, until the sauce has thickened, stirring all the time.
■ Stir in the tarragon and seasoning to taste, and then add the cream or soya cream*.
■ Toss the cooked pasta into the sauce and serve immediately with garlic bread or a mixed green salad.

Serves 4

TIP
■

Pasta is a marvellous convenience food. If you have unexpected guests for supper you can quickly make a sauce with store cupboard ingredients. Just chop and fry an onion in olive oil, add a pinch of dried oregano, a can of chopped tomatoes and a can of drained flageolet beans. Serve on a bed of pasta with freshly grated vegetarian cheese. Your guests will be impressed with your versatility!

FARFALLE WITH
MUSHROOMS AND SPINACH

*CAN BE VEGAN

Versatile pasta can be used as the basis for many quick but satisfying meals. This speedy dish with its interesting vegetables is ideal for informal entertaining.

225 g / 8 oz farfalle pasta
2 tablespoons olive oil
225 g / 8 oz mixed mushrooms, e.g. oyster, shiitake
    and field, thickly sliced
2 garlic cloves, crushed
100 g / 4 oz baby spinach leaves, washed and dried
6 sun-dried tomatoes in oil, finely chopped
salt and freshly ground black pepper

To garnish:
½ bunch fresh basil leaves
100 g / 4 oz cherry tomatoes, halved

■ Cook the pasta in lightly salted boiling water as instructed on the packet.
■ Meanwhile, heat the olive oil in a large frying pan. Quickly fry the mushrooms and garlic over a high heat for 2–3 minutes, until just cooked.
■ Add the baby spinach leaves and stir until wilted. Stir in the sun-dried tomatoes and seasoning to taste.
■ Drain the pasta and toss into the mushroom and spinach mixture. Turn into a serving dish, and serve garnished with torn fresh basil and cherry tomatoes.

Serves 4

TIP
■
A delicious addition to this recipe would be a tablespoon of (vegan) pesto, stirred in just before serving, and some toasted pine nuts sprinkled over the top. You can use different pasta shapes — the flat, ribbon-like tagliatelle works well with this mixture.

SUMMER
AND AL FRESCO ENTERTAINING

Left: Barbecue spread

BARBECUE MENU

■

Choose a selection from the following dishes to serve 4 people.

■

Spiced sweet potato slices

Beef tomatoes with balsamic vinegar marinade

Aubergine and Halloumi rolls

Peppers stuffed with tomatoes and feta cheese

Vegetable kebabs with oriental dressing

Tandoori-style paneer tikka kebabs

SUITABLE FOR VEGANS

SPICED SWEET
POTATO SLICES

You can vary the spice mixture used in this recipe to suit your own taste. It can also be brushed over raw slices of squash or aubergine and grilled in the same way.

2 large pink sweet potatoes, peeled and left whole
2 tablespoons olive oil
1/2 teaspoon ground coriander
1/2 teaspoon ground cumin
pinch of ground cardamom seeds
sea salt, to taste

■ Parboil the sweet potatoes for about 10 minutes, until just tender.
■ Allow to cool slightly and cut into 6-mm/1/4-in slices lengthways.
■ Mix the olive oil and spices together, brush them over the slices of sweet potato and then place over hot barbecue coals for a few minutes on each side until crisp and golden.
■ Sprinkle the spiced sweet potato slices with sea salt and serve immediately.

Serves 4

BEEF TOMATOES WITH
BALSAMIC VINEGAR MARINADE

SUITABLE FOR VEGANS

Easy, summery and Mediterranean, this dish uses the flavoursome large beef tomatoes. If you prefer, you could use smaller tomatoes straight from the garden, but reduce the cooking time a little.

4 ripe beef tomatoes
4 teaspoons balsamic vinegar
freshly ground black pepper
2 tablespoons olive oil
12 g / ½ oz fresh basil leaves
8 kalamata olives, to garnish

■ Cut the tomatoes in half, then make shallow criss-cross cuts over each cut side. Drizzle a little balsamic vinegar over each and season with black pepper. Leave to marinate for 30 minutes.

■ Brush both sides of each tomato half with olive oil, place skin-side down on the barbecue and grill gently until tender (about 10 minutes).

■ Sprinkle with extra balsamic vinegar, if liked, and scatter lots of torn fresh basil leaves over the top of each tomato. Chop the olives coarsely and scatter over the top of the tomatoes.

Serves 4

TIP
■
An alternative and very tasty marinade is to mix together 2 tablespoons of sunflower oil, 1 teaspoon of chilli oil (or 2 small dried chillies, crushed), 1 tablespoon of shoyu, 1 crushed garlic clove and 1 teaspoon of grated ginger. Season with black pepper. Make shallow criss-cross cuts on the tomato halves and drizzle over as before. Or mix a little honey, oil and lemon juice together and brush over the tomato halves. The sweetness of the honey brings out the flavour of the tomato.

AUBERGINE AND HALLOUMI ROLLS

This recipe or variations on it have been appearing on my barbecue for years. It now seems to be becoming a popular dish for all the TV cooks as well — so you know it's going to be good! The rolls can also be cooked easily on a conventional grill and served as a starter or finger food.

1 large aubergine
salt, for sprinkling
150 ml/¼ pint olive oil
freshly ground black pepper
8 teaspoons sun-dried tomato paste
8 basil leaves
225 g/8 oz Halloumi, cut into 8 pieces
16 wooden cocktail sticks, soaked in water for 30 minutes

■ Trim the end and slice the aubergine into 8 thin slices lengthways. Place on a baking tray and sprinkle with salt. Leave for 30–60 minutes, until the bitter juices have been extracted and the slices are pliable. Rinse the aubergine slices well and pat dry with kitchen paper.

■ Season the olive oil with freshly ground black pepper and brush over one side of each aubergine slice. Spread 1 teaspoon of sun-dried tomato paste over each slice, then place a basil leaf topped with a piece of Halloumi on one end of the aubergine slice and roll up. Secure by skewering with 2 criss-crossed cocktail sticks.

■ Brush the outside of the aubergine rolls with olive oil and barbecue for about 5–6 minutes on each side, until tender and starting to char.

Serves 4

BARBECUE TIPS

■

If you are using a 'traditional' barbecue, allow at least 30–45 minutes for the coals to become really hot before starting to cook. A gas barbecue is quicker but takes away some of the fun!

Buy long metal skewers for kebabs so that the handle ends are not over the coals and are easier to turn.

Long-handled tongs are useful for turning food, and a pair of oven gloves will stop you burning yourself when handling hot utensils.

PEPPERS STUFFED WITH
TOMATOES AND FETA CHEESE

Peppers, tomatoes and basil all complement each other. You can use sliced salad tomatoes in place of the sun-dried ones in this recipe, and ciabatta bread is wonderful for soaking up the juices.

4 red peppers
8 sun-dried tomatoes in oil
12 g / ½ oz fresh basil leaves, roughly torn
225 g / 8 oz feta cheese in oil
olive oil to drizzle
salt and freshly ground black pepper

- Halve the peppers lengthways through the stalk and remove the seeds.
- Place 1 sun-dried tomato in each half and sprinkle with half of the torn basil, reserving the rest for the garnish. Top with pieces of feta cheese.
- Drizzle each one with olive oil or a little of the oil from the tomatoes and cheese. Season with salt and freshly ground black pepper.
- Grill the stuffed peppers on the barbecue for about 10–15 minutes, until the peppers are cooked, the skin is charred and the cheese is starting to melt.
- Garnish with the reserved torn basil and serve with crusty garlic bread or bulgar wheat to soak up the juice.

Serves 4

TIP
▪

Salads complement barbecue food and, if fairly substantial, give your guests something to eat while the rest of the food is cooking. Try a tabbouleh (bulgar wheat salad), or quinoa with grilled courgettes and a minty vinaigrette and crumbled feta cheese. Pasta salads with lots of chopped, fresh vegetables and a vegan mayonnaise work well too. You can also cook some garlic bread in a foil parcel on the barbecue. Hand this round with the salad and use to soak up the marinade juices.

VEGETABLE KEBABS
WITH ORIENTAL DRESSING

TIP

■

These kebabs are also
good served with the
satay sauce on page 231.

This recipe is dairy free, but a delicious variation is to add
225 g/8 oz Halloumi cheese, cut into chunks and threaded onto
the skewers between the vegetables. Barbecues always seem to
involve a great deal of preparation, so to make things simpler, use one
of the ready flavoured packets of rice as an accompaniment — if you
feel you have time, you can make your own if you prefer.

1 medium courgette, cut into 16 slices
4 small onions or shallots, peeled
  and halved
1 yellow or orange pepper, deseeded
  and cut into 8 pieces
8 button mushrooms
4 cherry tomatoes
4 x 20-cm/8-in wooden skewers,
  soaked in water for 30 minutes
4 tablespoons olive oil
salt and freshly ground black pepper

Oriental dressing:
1 tablespoon shoyu

3 tablespoons cold-pressed
  sunflower oil
1 teaspoon fresh ginger juice (grate
  and squeeze juice out)
1 garlic clove, crushed
1 teaspoon toasted sesame oil
2 tablespoons fresh lime juice (or
  lemon if preferred)
salt and freshly ground black
  pepper

To serve:
225 g/8 oz ready flavoured Thai rice,
  cooked and chilled

■ Thread all the vegetables onto the wooden skewers, brush with olive oil
and season with salt and pepper. Grill over hot barbecue coals for about
10–15 minutes, turning frequently, until golden and tender.
■ Meanwhile, make the oriental dressing by beating all the ingredients
together and seasoning to taste.
■ Pour the dressing over the hot kebabs and serve with the chilled rice 'salad'.

Serves 4

TANDOORI-STYLE
PANEER TIKKA KEBABS

It is unusual to have a tandoori flavour in a vegetarian meal. Paneer is a firm Indian cheese which soaks up the flavour of the marinade and keeps its shape when cooked. This recipe is wonderful on a barbecue, but can also be cooked under a conventional grill if the weather changes. It makes a good starter for an Indian meal (see the Indian dinner party on page 235) or you can make smaller portions on cocktail sticks for party finger food.

150 ml/5 fl oz natural yogurt
juice of ½ lemon
1 tablespoon tandoori spice mix
200 g/7 oz paneer, cut into 24 cubes
1 green pepper, deseeded and cut
    into 16 pieces
8 small onions or shallots, peeled
    and halved
4 cherry tomatoes, halved

8 x 15-cm/6-in wooden skewers,
    soaked in water for 30 minutes
2 tablespoons groundnut oil

To serve:
4 pappads
shredded lettuce
cucumber and tomato slices
lemon quarters

■ Mix the yogurt, lemon juice and tandoori spice mix together in a shallow bowl. Add the cubes of paneer and stir to coat thoroughly. Cover and leave to marinate for 30–60 minutes (or overnight) in the refrigerator.

■ Thread the green pepper, paneer, onions and tomatoes onto each skewer. Brush with groundnut oil, place over hot coals and grill, turning frequently, until the vegetables and cheese are cooked and starting to char.
■ Grill the pappads as per the instructions on the packet. Serve the kebabs with the salad garnish, lemon quarters and pappads.

Serves 4

PICNIC MENU

■

*Choose a selection
from the following dishes
to serve 4 people.*

■

Aubergine,
courgette and
tomato cob

Crostini

Mint and butter
bean pâté

Roast vegetables
and goat's cheese
en croûte

Savoury tomato and
basil tatin

**SUITABLE FOR
VEGANS**

TIP

■

You can vary the filling in
this cob by adding a layer
of roasted peppers, a
selection of quickly fried
exotic mushrooms, some
wilted spinach or slices of
mozzarella or feta
cheese.

AUBERGINE,
COURGETTE AND TOMATO COB

This stuffed cob holds together to make a really colourful savoury
'gâteau' when cut into wedges. It is excellent for picnics as it is
easy to transport and keeps its shape.

1 white, round, crusty loaf, e.g. pain de campagne, or 4 individual crusty rolls
1 aubergine, sliced
3 tablespoons olive oil
1 large onion, sliced
2 garlic cloves, crushed
1 tablespoon brown sugar
225 g/8 oz courgettes, sliced
4 ripe tomatoes, skinned and sliced
1 tablespoon chopped fresh basil
1 tablespoon chopped fresh flat-leaf parsley
1 tablespoon chopped fresh oregano
salt and freshly ground black pepper

■ Preheat the oven to 200°C/400°F/Gas Mark 6.
■ Slice the top off the loaf or rolls and reserve. Remove the bread from the
inside, leaving just a shell.
■ Brush the aubergine slices with a little of the olive oil, place on a baking
sheet and bake in the preheated oven for about 15–20 minutes, until golden.
■ Heat the remaining olive oil in a frying pan. Fry the onion and garlic gently
for about 15 minutes, until turning golden and starting to caramelize. Stir in the
sugar and remove from the pan.
■ In the same pan, add a little more olive oil if necessary and fry the
courgettes until golden.
■ Layer half the aubergine, onion, courgettes, tomatoes and half the herbs
inside the bread shell, seasoning each layer. Repeat the layers and put the lid
on top. Wrap tightly in cling film and refrigerate for 2 hours or overnight.
The juices will soak into the bread. Cut into wedges to serve.

Serves 4

Opposite: Aubergine, courgette and tomato cob

*CAN BE VEGAN

CROSTINI

Crostini are small slices of bread, brushed with olive oil, toasted and topped with all manner of ingredients — the variety is as great as your imagination. All the elements of this recipe can be made 24 hours in advance.

12 slices day-old ciabatta bread
4–6 tablespoons olive oil
1 garlic clove, skinned and left whole

Mushroom topping:
50 g/2 oz button mushrooms, sliced
1 tablespoon olive oil
1 teaspoon herb vinegar
1 teaspoon mixed ground cumin
  and coriander
4 slices mozzarella cheese (omit
  for vegans*)

Mediterranean topping:
½ red onion, finely chopped
2 sun-dried tomatoes in oil, finely
  chopped
4 kalamata olives, stoned and
  chopped
1 teaspoon oregano, chopped
1 tablespoon olive oil
1 teaspoon balsamic vinegar
salt and freshly ground black pepper

Aubergine topping:
1 tablespoon olive oil
½ aubergine, finely chopped
2 ripe tomatoes, skinned and chopped
1 teaspoon basil leaves, torn
salt and freshly ground black pepper

■ Preheat the oven to 200°C/400°F/Gas Mark 6.
■ Brush each side of the slices of ciabatta bread with olive oil. Place on a baking tray and bake in the preheated oven for 10–15 minutes, until crisp and golden. Rub the clove of garlic over one side of each slice.
■ To make the mushroom topping, mix all the ingredients except the mozzarella together in a bowl. Leave to marinate for at least 30 minutes. Top 4 slices of the toast with the mixture and a slice of mozzarella cheese*, if using. Quickly melt the cheese under a hot grill before serving hot or cold.
■ For the Mediterranean topping, mix all the ingredients together and leave to marinate for at least 30 minutes. Use to top 4 slices of the toast.
■ For the aubergine topping, heat the olive oil in a pan and gently fry the aubergine until golden and tender. Stir in the tomatoes and basil and season to taste. Either top 4 slices of toast immediately and serve hot or, for a picnic, leave to cool and use the topping cold.

Serves 4

TIP

■

Although this recipe uses ciabatta bread, you could just as easily use thin slices of French stick prepared in the same way. If you don't like the flavour of raw garlic omit this from the recipe. The toppings given in this recipe are all cold and are therefore suitable for a picnic, but to make a change, add a little vegetarian mozzarella or Cheddar and pop them under the grill. Serve as appetizers when you are entertaining at home.

MINT AND BUTTER
BEAN PATE

Other pulses, such as flageolets, cannellini beans or canned broad beans, can be used in place of the butter beans in this delicious pâté. It can be turned into a dip by adding extra lemon juice and olive oil and a little tahini if liked (a variation on hummus). Serve with vegetable crudités (see page 212).

2 x 425-g/15-oz cans of butter beans, drained
grated zest and juice of 1 lemon
2 garlic cloves, crushed
2 tablespoons finely chopped fresh mint
4 tablespoons olive oil
4 tablespoons water (approx.)
salt and freshly ground black pepper
sprigs of mint, to garnish

To serve:
pitta bread triangles
mixed salad leaves and cherry tomatoes

■ Place the butter beans and lemon juice in a food processor and blend until smooth. Add the lemon zest, garlic, mint and olive oil, adjusting the amount of water to give a smooth pâté. Season to taste, then spoon the mixture into a serving dish or individual ramekins and garnish with mint sprigs.
■ Serve the butter bean pâté with warm pitta bread triangles and a salad garnish of lettuce and cherry tomatoes.

Serves 4

ROAST VEGETABLES
AND GOAT'S CHEESE EN CROUTE

The usual mixture of roast vegetables consists of roots, such as carrot, parsnip and sweet potato, or Mediterranean vegetables, such as aubergines and peppers. This recipe quickly roasts some of the more tender summer vegetables and uses the now popular goat's cheese to add extra flavour. If you find goat's cheese too strong, try using feta or even a crumbly Wensleydale instead.

100 g / 4 oz baby courgettes, quartered
50 g / 2 oz green beans, cut into 2.5-cm/1-in pieces
50 g / 2 oz mange tout, topped, tailed and halved
50 g / 2 oz fennel, chopped (optional)
50 g / 2 oz cherry tomatoes, halved

8 spring onions, quartered
8 garlic cloves, peeled and left whole
few sprigs of fresh rosemary
4 tablespoons olive oil
225 g / 8 oz puff pastry
100 g / 4 oz goat's cheese, sliced
salt and freshly ground black pepper
1 free-range egg, beaten

■ Preheat the oven to 200°C/400°F/Gas Mark 6.
■ Place all the prepared vegetables, including the spring onions and garlic, in a baking dish, together with the rosemary. Toss in the olive oil and bake, turning frequently, in the preheated oven for about 20 minutes, until starting to colour.
■ Remove from the oven and allow to cool. Remove the rosemary sprigs.
■ Roll out the puff pastry to make a square, 30 x 30 cm/12 x 12 in, and cut into 4 equal pieces, 15 x 15 cm/6 x 6 in. Place a quarter of the vegetable mixture on each pastry square. Top with the goat's cheese and season to taste.
■ Brush the edges of the pastry with egg and fold over into a triangle. Seal the edges well. Make a slit in the top of each package, and place on a baking tray. Brush with egg to glaze and bake in the preheated oven for about 20 minutes, until risen and golden. Serve warm or cold.

Serves 4

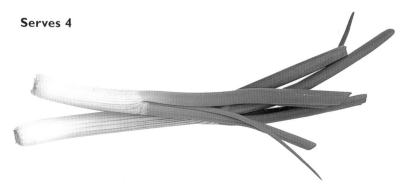

SAVOURY TOMATO
AND BASIL TATIN

These upside-down tarts were originally created by the Tatin sisters in France using caramelized apples topped with a rich pastry. The idea has become deservedly popular as it gives a lovely crisp pastry top which, when inverted, becomes the base. Try to get the sweet yellow cherry tomatoes for this recipe as they make an interesting contrast to the red.

200 g / 7 oz plain flour
pinch of salt
100 g / 4 oz vegan margarine
1 teaspoon dried basil
4–6 olives, finely chopped
4–6 tablespoons cold water
225 g / 8 oz onions, sliced
1 tablespoon olive oil

450 g / 1 lb ripe, flavoursome
    tomatoes, e.g. plum or beef, sliced
225 g / 8 oz yellow (or red) cherry
    tomatoes, halved
1 bunch fresh basil
salt and freshly ground black pepper
few olives, halved
basil leaves, to garnish

- Preheat the oven to 200°C/400°F/Gas Mark 6.
- Sift the flour and salt into a bowl. Rub in the margarine to resemble breadcrumbs. Stir in the basil and olives and enough water to make a firm dough. Roll into a ball, wrap in cling film and chill for 30 minutes.
- Meanwhile, fry the onions in the olive oil until starting to brown, then remove from the heat and allow to cool.
- Arrange the tomato slices and cherry tomato halves, cut-side down, in a decorative way on the base of a 20-cm/8-in solid-based cake tin. Reserve some of the basil leaves for the garnish and roughly tear the rest and sprinkle over the tomatoes. Season with salt and pepper and top with the onions.

- Roll out the pastry to fit and place over the onions. Cut to fit or push the edges in snugly. Bake for 20–25 minutes in the preheated oven until the pastry is crisp and golden. Cool for 5 minutes, then invert the tin and turn out onto a serving plate. Garnish with olives and basil leaves.

Serves 6

PICNIC TIPS
■

Try to provide food that can be eaten without knives and forks and which doesn't collapse between plate and mouth.

Over- rather than underestimate the food for a picnic — the fresh air always seems to sharpen the appetite and everyone will eat more than normal!

SUMMER MENU 1

∎

SERVES 4

∎

Sushi

Cous cous with summer vegetables

Beansprout salad with sesame dressing

Fresh summer fruit brûlée

(see page 251)

SUITABLE FOR VEGANS

SUSHI

It is now much easier to obtain Japanese ingredients and these chilled sushi make a light and summery starter. Watch out for the wasabi paste — it is much hotter than our native horseradish!

100 g/4 oz Arborio or other short-grain rice
2 teaspoons wasabi paste
4 tablespoons shoyu
a few pieces chopped, pickled ginger

Avocado filling:
1/2 avocado, peeled and sliced
1 tablespoon lemon juice
1 sheet nori (sea vegetable), toasted and cut into 1.25-cm/1/2-in strips
1 teaspoon wasabi paste (Japanese horseradish paste)

Red pepper filling:
1 sheet nori, toasted
1 tablespoon umeboshi sauce (plum)
1/4 red pepper, cut into thin strips
2.5-cm/1-in piece cucumber, cut into matchsticks

Ginger filling:
4 capers, finely chopped
few sprigs of fresh mint, finely chopped
16–20 slices pickled ginger in rice wine vinegar

∎ Cook the rice in boiling water, stirring occasionally to release the starch and make the rice sticky. Drain and cool until needed.

∎ For the avocado filling, take one-third of the cooked rice and form into 4 cubes. Toss the avocado slices in the lemon juice to stop them discolouring. Toast the nori over a gas flame for a few seconds, until it becomes green and translucent. Cut into strips. Take a cube of rice, put a little wasabi on top, then a slice of avocado and tie in place with a strip of nori. Chill.

∎ For the red pepper filling, place the toasted nori on a sushi mat or piece of cling film. Spread one-third of the rice over the nori. Make an indentation 1.25–2.5 cm/1/2–1 in in from one long edge with a chop stick, and spread with a little umeboshi sauce. Place the pepper and cucumber strips side by side along the indentation. Roll up firmly, using the mat or cling film to help you. Chill and cut into slices.

∎ For the ginger filling, take the remaining cooked rice and mix in the capers and fresh mint. Lay 4–5 pieces of pickled ginger onto a piece of cling film, put a heaped tablespoon of the rice mixture in the centre and bring the ginger up around to enclose it. Use the cling film to compress the ball by gathering tightly and twisting. Refrigerate until ready to serve. Repeat 3 more times.

∎ To serve: arrange a selection of sushi on each plate with 1/2 teaspoon of wasabi paste, a small bowl containing 1 tablespoon of shoyu and a little pile of chopped pickled ginger.

Opposite: Sushi

Cous cous
WITH SUMMER VEGETABLES

WINE SUGGESTIONS
■
White
Entre Deux Mers
Château la Blanquerie
Fruity dry white Bordeaux

Red
Merlot del Veneto Pelage
*A soft and smooth
Italian red*

During the summer months it is wonderful to be able to use the new produce when it is young, crisp and full of flavour — much better than the woody or watery vegetables that are found on the supermarket shelves when they are full grown. This recipe makes full use of these delightful vegetables and the cous cous absorbs the flavour of the dressing.

225 g / 8 oz cous cous
100 g / 4 oz baby carrots, topped and tailed
100 g / 4 oz baby courgettes, topped, tailed and halved
100 g / 4 oz mange tout, topped, tailed and halved
4 tablespoons olive oil
8 shallots or small onions, quartered

1 stick celery, sliced
2 tablespoons white wine vinegar
grated zest of 1 lemon
1 tablespoon chopped fresh coriander
salt and freshly ground black pepper
100 g / 4 oz cherry tomatoes
25 g / 1 oz pine nuts, toasted
coriander leaves, to garnish

■ Place the cous cous in a bowl. Pour boiling water over and leave to stand for 15 minutes. Drain off any excess water, cool and spoon into a serving dish.

■ Steam the baby carrots, courgettes and mange tout until just tender. Put 1 tablespoon of the olive oil in a saucepan and quickly fry the shallots or baby onions until golden brown. Add the celery and cook for 2 minutes. Remove from the heat and allow to cool.

■ Mix the remaining olive oil with the vinegar and lemon zest. Add the chopped coriander and season well.

■ Mix all the vegetables and cherry tomatoes together, toss in the vinaigrette and spoon over the top of the cous cous. Top with the toasted pine nuts and serve garnished with coriander leaves.

BEANSPROUT SALAD
WITH SESAME DRESSING

This is a fresh and summery salad with an oriental touch. If you grow your own chives, use some of the edible flower heads for a pretty garnish; they make an interesting talking point.

½ head of Chinese leaves, finely shredded
100 g/4 oz baby spinach leaves, washed and coarsely chopped
100 g/4 oz beansprouts
4 spring onions, shredded
50 g/2 oz baby sweetcorn, halved lengthways
50 g/2 oz mange tout, topped, tailed and blanched

1 tablespoon sesame seeds
few chives, chopped, for garnish

For the dressing:
2 tablespoons rice wine vinegar
1 tablespoon sunflower or groundnut oil
1 teaspoon toasted sesame oil
salt and freshly ground black pepper

■ Prepare the Chinese leaves, spinach, beansprouts, spring onions, sweetcorn and mange tout, and mix together in a large bowl.

■ Mix the dressing ingredients together, then pour over the salad. Toss well and arrange on a large platter.

■ Dry toast the sesame seeds in a non-stick pan. Sprinkle over the top of the salad. Serve garnished with chopped chives.

TIP
■

Chinese bean sprouts are sprouted mung beans, but many other pulses and seeds can be sprouted successfully. Place about 2 tablespoons into a wide-necked jar with muslin over the top. Rinse and drain thoroughly twice a day. Try green lentils or fenugreek seeds for a slightly spicy flavour, or alfalfa seeds for the fresh taste of baby peas.

SUMMER MENU 2

■

SERVES 4

■

Sweet and sour
peppers

Lemony bean salad

Mixed tomato salad

Italian spinach and
ricotta gnocchi

Nectarine and
physalis cream pie
(see page 250)

*CAN BE VEGAN

SWEET AND SOUR
BAKED PEPPERS

The combination of vinegar and honey (or maple syrup) brings out the natural flavours of this dish. It can be eaten as an appetizer or a main dish, and can even be served on a bed of pasta.

5 tablespoons olive oil
1 large onion, sliced
2 garlic cloves, crushed
4 mixed colour peppers, deseeded and sliced
225 g/8 oz ripe tomatoes, skinned and chopped
2 tablespoons red wine vinegar
1 tablespoon honey or maple syrup*
1 tablespoon tomato purée
salt and freshly ground black pepper

To serve:
1 tablespoon balsamic vinegar
1/2 bunch fresh basil leaves, torn
12 olives, stoned and halved
crusty white bread

■ Preheat the oven to 200°C/400°F/Gas Mark 6.
■ Use one tablespoon of the olive oil to fry the onion and garlic until just soft. Mix in all the other ingredients, season and turn into an ovenproof dish.
■ Bake in the preheated oven for 40–50 minutes, basting occasionally, until the peppers are browning in patches. Remove from the oven and serve sprinkled with balsamic vinegar, freshly torn basil and olives, with crusty white bread.

LEMONY BEAN SALAD

This substantial salad can be served as a starter with crusty bread. It is also good for barbecues.

100 g/4 oz baby spinach leaves, washed
425 g/15 oz can flageolet beans, rinsed and drained
2 ripe avocados, peeled, stoned and sliced
1 red onion, finely chopped
1–2 tablespoons sunflower seeds

For the dressing:
juice and finely chopped zest of 1 lemon
2 tablespoons fruity extra virgin olive oil
apple juice concentrate, to taste
1 teaspoon Dijon mustard
salt and freshly ground black pepper

- Arrange the baby spinach leaves on a platter. Mix the prepared flageolet beans, avocados and red onion together and arrange on top of the spinach.
- Mix the dressing ingredients together and drizzle over the salad.
- Dry toast the sunflower seeds in a pan and scatter over the top.

TIPS FOR SUMMER ENTERTAINING
■

Summer is always a good time of year for entertaining and it is a good idea to prepare as much as possible in advance and then serve it cold.

Keep the cooking simple to avoid spending too much time in the kitchen.

MIXED TOMATO SALAD

A simple, but colourful salad of different tomatoes, which will complement many summer flavours.

4 beef tomatoes, washed and thinly sliced
225 g/8 oz cherry tomatoes, halved
8 sun-dried tomatoes in oil, finely chopped
150 g/5 oz mozzarella cheese (omit for vegan*)
handful of fresh basil
few sprigs of fresh oregano

fresh edible flowers, to garnish

For the dressing:
2 tablespoons oil from the sun-dried tomatoes
2 teaspoons balsamic vinegar
1 tablespoon white wine vinegar
salt and freshly ground black pepper

- Arrange the sliced beef tomato on a platter. Scatter the cherry tomato halves and sun-dried tomatoes over the top.
- Cut the mozzarella into tiny chunks and scatter over the tomatoes (if using).
- Mix the dressing ingredients together and drizzle over the tomatoes and cheese.
- Use the basil and oregano leaves and edible flowers to decorate the salad.

ITALIAN SPINACH
AND RICOTTA GNOCCHI

**WINE
SUGGESTIONS**
■

White
Pino Grigio del Veneto
Pelage
*Aromatic and lively off-dry
Italian white*

Red
Volcanic Hills Kekfrankos
*A light and friendly
Hungarian red*

It can be difficult to get a good vegetarian Parmesan and you will often find that a vegetarian Pecorino is a much tastier alternative.

200 g/7 oz baby spinach leaves
150 g/5 oz ricotta cheese
50 g/2 oz plain white flour
60 g/2½ oz vegetarian Pecorino or
  Parmesan, grated
1 free-range egg yolk
pinch of nutmeg
salt and freshly ground black pepper
extra Pecorino or Parmesan, grated

For the tomato sauce:
1 tablespoon olive oil

1 small red onion, finely chopped
1 small piece fennel or celery, finely
  chopped (optional)
1 garlic clove, crushed
450 g/1 lb fresh tomatoes, skinned,
  deseeded and chopped
150 ml/¼ pint white wine
4 sun-dried tomatoes in oil, chopped
2 tablespoons chopped fresh
  flat-leaf parsley
salt and freshly ground black
  pepper

■ First, make the tomato sauce. Heat the oil in a saucepan, add the onion, fennel or celery, if using, and the garlic and cook gently until tender. Add the fresh tomatoes and white wine and bring to the boil. Simmer for about 10 minutes, until starting to reduce and thicken. Stir in the sun-dried tomatoes, parsley and seasoning to taste. Keep warm.

■ Wash the spinach and cook for 1–2 minutes in a covered pan in just the water left clinging to the leaves. Turn into a sieve and press down well to remove as much liquid as possible. Chop the drained spinach.

■ Beat the spinach into the ricotta cheese, together with the flour, 60 g/2½ oz of the Pecorino or Parmesan and enough egg yolk to bind. Season well with nutmeg, salt and pepper.

■ Use floured hands to help you shape the mixture, about 1 teaspoon at a time, into little balls. Bring a large pan of water to the boil and drop batches of the gnocchi into the simmering water. Cook for 3–4 minutes, until they float on the surface. Remove with a slotted spoon and place in a greased ovenproof dish.

■ Pour the sauce over the gnocchi and sprinkle with some grated cheese. Place under a hot grill until the cheese has melted, then serve immediately.

Opposite: Italian spinach and ricotta gnocchi

SUMMER MENU 3

■

SERVES 4

■

Stuffed baked tomatoes with olives

Penne tossed with artichokes and mozzarella

Lemon mille feuilles
(see page 260)

SUITABLE FOR VEGANS

STUFFED BAKED
TOMATOES WITH OLIVES

A very simple starter, these tomatoes can be served either hot or chilled, with some crusty bread.

4 tablespoons bulgar wheat
4 large tomatoes
1 tablespoon olive oil
1 small onion, finely chopped
1 garlic clove, crushed
50 g /2 oz oyster mushrooms, chopped
4 tablespoons sweetcorn kernels (canned or frozen)
4 sun-dried tomatoes in oil, chopped
8 kalamata olives, stoned and finely chopped
1 tablespoon chopped oregano or basil
salt and freshly ground black pepper
sprigs of parsley, to garnish

■ Preheat the oven to 190°C/375°F/Gas Mark 5.
■ Put the bulgar wheat in a bowl and pour boiling water over to cover. Leave to soak for 15–20 minutes, until tender. Drain off any excess water.
■ Cut the tops off the tomatoes and reserve. Scoop out the seeds and some of the flesh. Turn upside-down on kitchen paper to drain.
■ Heat the olive oil and fry the onion and garlic until tender. Add the oyster mushrooms and fry for 2 minutes. Stir in the sweetcorn, sun-dried tomatoes, olives, bulgar wheat and herbs and season well.
■ Pack the filling into the tomatoes and top each with a tomato 'lid'. Place in a greased ovenproof dish and bake in the preheated oven for 30–40 minutes. Serve either hot or cooled, garnished with parsley sprigs.

Serves 4

PENNE TOSSED WITH
ARTICHOKES AND MOZZARELLA

This dish is tasty with or without the mozzarella cheese. It is quick to cook so it doesn't involve staying in a hot kitchen for too long, making it ideal for summer entertaining.

225 g /8 oz penne pasta
400-g /14-oz can of artichoke hearts
3 tablespoons olive oil
400-g /14-oz can of chopped tomatoes
12 black olives, stoned and roughly chopped
2 tablespoons vegan pesto
salt and freshly ground black pepper
150 g /5 oz mozzarella cheese, sliced (omit for vegans*)
few sprigs of fresh basil, to garnish

■ Cook the pasta as instructed on the packet until tender but still firm (*al dente*). Drain well.

■ Meanwhile, drain and quarter the artichoke hearts, place on a grill pan and drizzle with 2 tablespoons of olive oil. Grill, turning occasionally, until golden.

■ Heat the remaining olive oil in a saucepan, add the chopped tomatoes, black olives and pesto and cook for 2 minutes. Stir in the grilled artichokes and season to taste with salt and pepper.

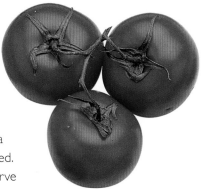

■ Toss in the cooked pasta, turn into an ovenproof dish and top with mozzarella, if using. Place under a hot grill until the mozzarella has melted. Garnish with fresh basil leaves and serve with a salad.

DRINKS TIP
■

For those of you wanting non-alcoholic drinks, some elderflower cordial mixed to taste with soda water is wonderfully refreshing on a hot sunny day.

WINE SUGGESTIONS
■

White
Volcanic Hills Harslevelu
Deep flavoured Hungarian with a hint of spice

Red
Chianti San Vito
Medium bodied, fresh and well rounded

CHRISTMAS
AND WINTER ENTERTAINING

Left: Chocolate, brandy and hazelnut yule log (page 196), and Mushroom-stuffed filo parcels (page 192)

*CAN BE VEGAN

PEAR, CELERIAC
AND STILTON SOUP

Celeriac always seems to be the poor relation of the root vegetables as people tend to look at its knobbly exterior and shy away from experimenting with it. This is a pity as it has a slightly sweet celery flavour and purées to a beautifully smooth texture. If you cannot obtain celeriac, then try using a squash instead.

675 g/1 ½ lb pears, peeled and cored
2 tablespoons sunflower oil
1 onion, chopped
450 g/1 lb celeriac, peeled and roughly chopped
1.2 litres/2 pints vegetable stock
salt and freshly ground black pepper
175–225 g/6–8 oz vegetarian Stilton cheese, crumbled (omit for vegans*)
single cream or soya cream*, to serve
chopped chives, to garnish

■ Cut the pears into slices and poach them in 300 ml/½ pint water until they are tender. Blend the pears and water together and reserve.
■ Heat the oil in a large saucepan and gently fry the onion until translucent.
■ Add the celeriac and cook, covered, for 10–15 minutes, or until tender.
■ Add the vegetable stock and blended pears, bring to the boil and then reduce the heat and simmer for 10 minutes.
■ Liquidize the soup in a blender or food processor and return to a clean pan. Reheat gently, season to taste and stir in the crumbled Stilton*, if using.
■ Serve immediately with a swirl of dairy or soya cream* and a sprinkling of chopped chives.

FESTIVE CHESTNUT
BREAD ROLLS

These rolls complement the fruit flavours in the Pear, Celeriac and Stilton Soup (opposite), and the Apple, Mushroom and Calvados Soup (see page 197). They are also delicious with cheese.

175 g/6 oz strong wholemeal flour
175 g/6 oz strong white flour
$\frac{1}{2}$ teaspoon salt
$\frac{1}{2}$ teaspoon ground nutmeg or cinnamon
12 g/$\frac{1}{2}$ oz fresh yeast (or 1 teaspoon dried yeast)
2 teaspoons sugar
240 ml/8 fl oz (approx.) hand-hot water
100 g/4 oz chestnuts (cooked weight), chopped
dairy or soya milk*, to glaze

■ Preheat the oven to 220°C/425°F/Gas Mark 7.
■ Mix the flours, salt and the nutmeg or cinnamon together in a large mixing bowl. Cream the yeast and sugar together and add a little hand-hot water. Mix well and leave in a warm place for 5 minutes, until frothy.
■ Pour the yeast mixture over the flour in the bowl and add enough water, one tablespoon at a time, to make a stiff, but not sticky, dough.
■ Tip the dough out onto a floured work surface and knead for 10 minutes. Place the dough in a clean, lightly oiled bowl, cover with a clean tea towel or loose cling film and leave in a warm place until doubled in size (about 1 hour).
■ Punch the dough down, turn out onto a floured surface, add the chopped chestnuts and knead for 5 minutes, making sure that the chestnuts are evenly distributed throughout the mixture.
■ Divide into 6 balls and shape into rolls. Allow to prove by leaving the rolls in a warm place for 20–30 minutes, until well risen. Glaze with dairy or soya milk* and bake for 15–20 minutes in the preheated oven. If the the rolls sound hollow when tapped on the base, then they are cooked.

Makes 6 rolls

MUSHROOM-STUFFED
FILO PARCELS

Use your favourite vegetarian stuffing mix in this recipe or make your own. This recipe is excellent for Christmas in a family that has only one or two vegetarian members or is perhaps entertaining a vegetarian guest. The parcels can be assembled and then refrigerated for 24 hours before cooking them and completing the dish. Indeed, most of the ingredients will be part of everyone's Christmas meal.

TIP

▪

A tasty alternative filling is to top the mushrooms with a piece of vegetarian Brie in place of the stuffing, and then top this with the cranberry or redcurrant sauce. In the summer, you could fill each mushroom with ricotta and spinach and top with a teaspoon of peach chutney to give a Mediterranean flavour to the parcels.

6 medium-sized field mushrooms (flat)
oil to fry the mushrooms
225 g / 8 oz packet fresh or frozen
    filo pastry
25 g / 1 oz butter or vegan
    margarine*, melted
6 teaspoons cranberry or
    redcurrant sauce
extra cranberry or redcurrant
    sauce, to serve

Hazelnut stuffing:
1 packet vegetarian stuffing mix,
    e.g. parsley, lemon and thyme
1 small onion, finely chopped
1 stick celery, finely chopped
15 g / ½ oz butter or vegan
    margarine*
25–50 g / 1–2 oz roasted hazelnuts,
    chopped
milk, dairy or soya*, for binding

▪ Preheat the oven to 190°C/375°F/Gas Mark 5.
▪ Fry the mushrooms for 3–4 minutes on each side until tender, then cool. Make up the stuffing mix of your choice. Fry the onion and celery in the butter or margarine*, and then add the stuffing mix and hazelnuts. Add a little milk (dairy or soya*) if necessary to bind together. Leave to cool.
▪ Fill each flat field mushroom with the stuffing mixture.
▪ Take 3 sheets of filo pastry at a time. Cut them in half so that you have 10–12.5-cm/4–5-in squares. Take one square and brush with a little melted butter or margarine. Place another square on top at an angle, and brush again. Do the same with a third sheet.
▪ Place a stuffed mushroom in the middle of the filo pastry, and top with a teaspoon of cranberry or redcurrant sauce. Bring the edges of the pastry up together and pinch them to form a little parcel (money-bag shape). Make up the rest of the parcels in the same way.
▪ Brush with melted butter or margarine* and place on a greased baking tray. Bake in the preheated oven for 15–20 minutes, until the pastry is crisp and golden. Serve hot with extra cranberry or redcurrant sauce.

ORANGE CARROTS
AND SWEET POTATOES

*CAN BE VEGAN

As Christmas is a special occasion, it's always a good idea to use some slightly more exotic or unusual vegetables to accompany the festive dinner. This dish makes a delicious change from the traditional brussels sprouts and roasted parsnips.

450 g / 1 lb sweet potatoes, peeled
15 g / ½ oz butter or vegan margarine*
175 ml / 6 fl oz orange juice
2.5-cm / 1-in piece of root ginger, peeled, grated and juice squeezed out
grated zest of ½ orange
450 g / 1 lb carrots, peeled and cut into matchsticks
salt and freshly ground black pepper
chopped parsley, to garnish

■ Parboil the sweet potatoes in boiling lightly salted water for 10 minutes, then drain and cut into cubes.
■ Melt the butter or margarine* in a saucepan. Add the orange juice, ginger juice, orange zest, sweet potatoes and carrots. Bring to the boil. Reduce the heat, cover the pan and simmer for 8–10 minutes, until the vegetables are tender.
■ Remove the pan lid, turn up the heat and boil the liquid in the pan until syrupy, stirring frequently. Season to taste with salt and freshly ground black pepper.
■ Transfer the glazed vegetables to a warm serving dish and sprinkle with chopped parsley.

Below: Mushroom-stuffed filo parcels

ROAST POTATOES
AND PARSNIPS

By parboiling the potatoes and then roughening the flat side with a fork, they become very crispy when roasted, whereas the onion rings become slightly charred.

6 medium potatoes, peeled and halved lengthways
4 parsnips, peeled and sliced
good pinch of dried mixed herbs
2 onions, cut into thin rings
4–6 tablespoons sunflower or olive oil
salt and freshly ground black pepper
225 g/8 oz cherry tomatoes

■ Preheat the oven to 200°C/400°F/Gas Mark 6.
■ Parboil the potatoes for 10 minutes until the outsides are slightly soft. Drain and place in a roasting tin flat side up. Use a fork to roughen the flat uppermost side of the potato.
■ Add the prepared parsnips, sprinkle with mixed herbs and arrange the onion rings over the top. Drizzle with sunflower or olive oil and season with salt and lots of black pepper.
■ Roast for 40 minutes, basting several times, then add the cherry tomatoes and bake for a further 15–20 minutes, until all the vegetables are cooked and the tomatoes have split open.
■ Serve the roast vegetables with steamed broccoli, brussels sprouts or mange tout with your Christmas meal.

WINE SUGGESTIONS
■

White
Estate Chardonnay, Millton Estate
Rich and ripe New Zealand dry white

Red
Valréas Côtes du Rhône Villages
Award winning spicy red with great structure

BREAD SAUCE
WITH ROASTED GARLIC

Adding creamed roasted garlic to this traditional accompaniment to Christmas dinner lifts it out of the ordinary. Your guests will be trying to guess the mystery ingredient.

TIP

■

This sauce can be made in advance and frozen until required.

1 head of garlic
3 tablespoons olive oil
6 cloves
1 onion, peeled and left whole
1 bay leaf
6 whole peppercorns
300 ml/½ pint milk (dairy or soya*)
50 g/2 oz fresh white breadcrumbs
15 g/½ oz butter or vegan margarine*
salt and freshly ground black pepper
grated nutmeg
2 tablespoons cream (omit for vegan*)

■ Preheat the oven to 200°C/400°F/Gas Mark 6.
■ Break the garlic into cloves, leaving the skin on. Place in a small ovenproof dish, drizzle with olive oil and bake in the oven for 15–20 minutes, until tender when pierced with a knife. Remove from the oven and leave to cool.
■ Stick the cloves into the onion and place in a saucepan with the bay leaf, peppercorns and milk (dairy or soya*). Bring to the boil, then take the pan off the heat and add the breadcrumbs. Stir in the butter or margarine* and leave to stand for 30 minutes.
■ Squeeze the garlic out of their skins and mash until you have a creamy textured purée.
■ Remove the peppercorns, onion and bay leaf from the sauce, and stir in the creamed garlic. Season to taste with salt, pepper and nutmeg and stir in the cream (omit for vegan*), if using. Reheat gently to serve.

CHOCOLATE, BRANDY
AND HAZELNUT YULE LOG

If the thought of rolling a roulade is too complicated for you, leave the sponge to cool, trim the edges and cut into three pieces. Divide the brandy cream and cherries into four and layer up the sponge with cream and cherries in between. Top with cream and use the last portion to pipe rosettes around the edge. Decorate with cherry halves and grated chocolate.

For the roulade:
175 g/6 oz plain chocolate
2 tablespoons brandy
5 free-range eggs, separated
175 g/6 oz caster sugar
100 g/4 oz hazelnuts, roasted
icing sugar, for dusting

For the filling:
1–2 tablespoons brandy
300 ml/½ pint double cream, whipped
425-g/15-oz can of black cherries,
    drained, stoned and halved
icing sugar, for dusting
sprig of holly

■ Preheat the oven to 190°C/375°F/Gas Mark 5. Line a 33 x 23-cm/13 x 9-in Swiss roll tin with non-stick baking parchment.
■ Melt the chocolate in a bowl over a saucepan of simmering water. Stir in the brandy and leave to cool a little.
■ Whisk the egg yolks and sugar in a large bowl, again over a pan of simmering water, until the mixture becomes thick and creamy.
■ Combine the cooled chocolate and egg yolk mixture. Grind the hazelnuts and fold in the chocolate mixture.
■ In a grease-free bowl, whisk the egg whites until stiff. Fold into the chocolate mixture with a metal spoon until no whites can be seen.
■ Pour into the prepared Swiss roll tin and spread evenly. Cook in the preheated oven for 20–25 minutes, until the sponge springs back when lightly pressed.
■ Lay a sheet of baking parchment on a wire cooling tray and turn the roulade out onto it. Cover with a clean damp tea towel before peeling off the lining parchment. Trim the edges.
■ Transfer the roulade and parchment to the work top. Roll up the roulade with the parchment inside and leave to rest for 5 minutes.
■ Fold the brandy into the cream. Unroll the roulade and spread the cream over the surface, leaving a 1.5-cm/½-in gap along one long edge. Scatter with the cherries and roll up. Dust with icing sugar and decorate with holly.

Serves 6–8

APPLE, MUSHROOM
AND CALVADOS SOUP

Calvados, the apple brandy from Normandy, gives a boost to the slightly sweet and fruity flavour of this unusual soup. Ordinary brandy can be substituted if preferred.

2 tablespoons groundnut oil
225 g /8 oz onions, finely chopped
225 g /8 oz potatoes, finely chopped
225 g /8 oz mushrooms, chopped
600 ml /1 pint vegetable stock
300 ml /½ pint apple juice
salt and freshly ground black pepper
4–6 tablespoons Calvados (or brandy)
single cream or soya cream* to serve

■ Heat the oil in a saucepan and fry the onions until starting to brown. Add the potatoes and mushrooms and cook gently for 5 minutes.
■ Add the stock and apple juice, bring to the boil and simmer for 20–30 minutes. Allow to cool and then blend until smooth in a blender or food processor.
■ Return the puréed soup to a clean pan and gently reheat. Season and stir in the Calvados. Serve garnished with a swirl of cream.

WINTER MENU I

■

SERVES 4

■

Apple, mushroom and Calvados soup

Griddled aubergine stacks

Exotic fruit tatin with butterscotch sauce

*CAN BE VEGAN

GRIDDLED
AUBERGINE STACKS

This recipe is completely dairy free, but if you like cheese these vegetable stacks are lovely topped with a slice of griddled Halloumi. The sauce should be dotted with lots of tiny pieces of tomato and pepper, which form the 'confetti'.

a little olive oil
1 large aubergine, cut into rings
2 beef tomatoes, skinned and cut into rings
zest of 1 lemon, finely chopped
few sprigs of fresh sage, chopped
few sprigs of fresh thyme, chopped
few fresh chives, finely chopped
salt and freshly ground black pepper
balsamic vinegar, to taste
4 slices Halloumi cheese
lemon zest, to garnish
chives or chive flowers, to garnish

Tomato confetti sauce:
1 tablespoon olive oil
1 small onion, finely chopped
1 garlic clove, crushed
225 g /8 oz fresh, ripe, full-flavoured tomatoes, skinned and finely chopped
150 ml /¼ pint vegetarian white wine
1 yellow or red pepper, roasted, skin removed and cut into strips, then across into diamonds
1 teaspoon balsamic vinegar
salt and pepper

■ First, make the sauce. Heat the olive oil in a saucepan and fry the onion gently with the garlic. Add half of the chopped tomatoes and the white wine and cook for 5 minutes. Blend until smooth. Mix in the rest of the chopped tomatoes with the pepper pieces and 1 teaspoon of balsamic vinegar. Season to taste.

■ Brush the griddle with olive oil and cook the aubergine slices so that they are seared with stripes. Put on one side and keep warm. Grill the beef tomato slices gently.

■ Mix the lemon and herbs together and season well. On individual serving plates, layer the aubergine, tomato and herb mix. Drizzle with a little balsamic vinegar. Repeat until all the layers are used up and top with a slice of tomato and a sprinkling of the herb mixture. Grill the slices of Halloumi and arrange on top of each stack, garnished with lemon zest and chives. Drizzle tomato confetti sauce around the plate and decorate with chives or chive flowers. Serve warm.

Opposite: Griddled aubergine stacks

*CAN BE VEGAN

EXOTIC FRUIT TATIN
WITH BUTTERSCOTCH SAUCE

The original Tatin or 'upside down tart' was made with apples, but you can vary the fruits or even make a savoury version (see page 177). By cooking the pastry on top of the fruit and then turning it out so that the pastry becomes the base you achieve a crisp rather than a soggy crust with the fruit in a thick syrup. Add the rich butterscotch sauce for anyone with a really sweet tooth and/or dairy or soya cream to complete this dessert.

TIP

The pastry crust can be made very quickly in a food processor. Add just enough water to the rest of the ingredients to form a ball which comes away from the sides of the processor bowl. Then rest in the refrigerator and continue as before.

Use a solid-based cake tin. The juices will leak out of a loose-based tin.

50 g/2 oz butter or vegan margarine*
225 g/8 oz fresh pineapple, sliced
1 ripe mango, sliced
1 banana, cut into rings
2–3 tablespoons dark muscovado sugar
1 tablespoon rum
partially opened physalis (optional)
icing sugar, for dusting
dairy cream or soya cream*

Pastry crust:
100 g/4 oz plain white flour
pinch of cinnamon or mixed spice
50 g/2 oz butter or vegan margarine*
7–8 tablespoons iced water

Butterscotch sauce (not vegan):
75 g/3 oz butter
200 g/7 oz dark muscovado sugar
2 tablespoons golden syrup
75 ml/3 fl oz double cream

■ Preheat the oven to 200°C/400°F/Gas Mark 6.

■ Make the pastry: sift the flour and spice into a bowl. Cut the butter or margarine* into small pieces, then rub in with the fingertips to a breadcrumb consistency. Add sufficient water to mix to a dough. Roll into a ball, wrap in cling film and refrigerate for 30 minutes.

■ For the topping: melt the butter or margarine* in a frying pan and gently fry all the fruit until just tender. Stir in the sugar until melted. Take off the heat, stir in the rum and leave to cool. Place the fruit mixture in a 21-cm/8½-in round non-stick, solid-based, shallow cake tin.

■ Roll out the pastry crust dough, cover the fruit and trim the edges to fit. Bake in the preheated oven for about 20 minutes, until golden.

■ Turn out by inverting the tatin onto a serving plate. Decorate with physalis and icing sugar and serve with butterscotch sauce, cream or soya cream*.

■ To make the butterscotch sauce, melt the butter, sugar and syrup in a small pan over a gentle heat, stirring all the time. Stir in the cream and serve.

WARM AVOCADO
SALAD WITH RED PEPPER DRESSING

Avocados are usually served cold, but frying them quickly develops the flavour and adds a new dimension. You could also drizzle a mixture of olive oil, raspberry vinegar and a dash of balsamic vinegar over the top for a summery variation to this dish.

1 red pepper
2 garlic cloves, left whole with skins intact
olive oil, to drizzle
50 g/2 oz ground almonds
5 tablespoons extra virgin olive oil
1 tablespoon Dijon mustard
1 tablespoon balsamic vinegar
1 tablespoon chopped fresh coriander
150 ml/¼ pint dry white wine
salt and freshly ground black pepper
2 large ripe avocados, peeled and stoned
1 packet mixed salad leaves
fresh coriander, to garnish

■ Preheat the oven to 200°C/400°F/Gas Mark 6.
■ Place the red pepper and whole cloves of garlic on a baking sheet and drizzle with olive oil. Roast until the pepper skin is starting to blacken and char and the garlic is soft when pierced with a knife. Remove the skin and seeds from the pepper, retaining the juices, and squeeze the garlic out of the skins.
■ Blend the red pepper flesh, reserved juice, garlic, ground almonds, 3 tablespoons of the olive oil, mustard, vinegar and coriander together until smooth.
■ Add the wine and blend until the desired consistency is reached. Season to taste, pour into a saucepan and set aside.
■ Cut the avocados in half and then into slices. Heat the remaining olive oil in a non-stick frying pan and, when hot, quickly toss the avocados in the oil until heated through but not soft.
■ Heat the sauce gently over low heat. Meanwhile, arrange the mixed salad leaves on 4 serving plates with the avocado slices on top. Drizzle the warm sauce over them and serve garnished with fresh coriander leaves.

WINTER MENU 2
■
SERVES 4
■

Warm avocado salad with red pepper dressing

Rosti stacks with spicy peach coulis

Warm puy lentil salad

Red cabbage and onion salad

Panettone bread and butter pudding

SUITABLE FOR VEGANS

ROSTI STACKS
WITH SPICY PEACH COULIS

Although there are several elements to this dish, it is relatively easy to prepare and each stage can be made in advance and then refrigerated. The spicy peach coulis is an unusual contrasting taste.

2 large potatoes
350 g/12 oz celeriac or parsnips
pinch of ground nutmeg
salt and freshly ground black pepper
3 tablespoons olive oil
2 onions, sliced
1 tablespoon soft brown sugar
225 g/8 oz mushrooms, sliced
1 garlic clove, crushed
fresh parsley and basil leaves, to
    garnish

Gremolata:
50 g/2 oz vegan margarine, softened

1 garlic clove, crushed
juice and zest of ½ lemon
few sprigs of fresh parsley, chopped
few sprigs of fresh basil, chopped
salt and freshly ground black
    pepper

Spicy peach coulis:
2 small onions, very finely chopped
1 tablespoon olive oil
1–2 tablespoons mild curry
    powder
225 g/8 oz peach chutney
4–5 tablespoons water

■ Preheat the oven to 200°C/400°F/Gas Mark 6.
■ Peel the potatoes and celeriac or parsnips. Halve the potatoes and cut the celeriac into similar-sized pieces. Par-boil for 5 minutes (if using parsnips, leave raw), then drain and coarsely grate. Season with the nutmeg, salt and pepper.
■ Grease a baking sheet and arrange the mixed grated vegetables in four 10-cm/4-in mounds. Flatten with a spatula and make a depression in the centre, drizzle with a little olive oil, then bake for 25–30 minutes, until golden.
■ Meanwhile, fry the onions in 1 tablespoon olive oil until golden brown, then stir in the sugar and seasoning. Remove from the heat and keep warm. Cook the mushrooms and garlic in the remaining olive oil for 5 minutes. Season and keep warm.
■ Make the gremolata by beating all the ingredients until well blended.
■ Take the rostis out of the oven. Top with the onions, then the mushrooms and finally the gremolata. Return to the oven for 10 minutes to heat through.
■ Meanwhile, make the coulis. Gently fry the onions in the oil until tender, add the curry powder and cook for 2 minutes, stirring all the time. Add the chutney and water and heat through gently. Blend until smooth.
■ Place the rostis on serving plates and pour a little coulis around each one. Garnish with fresh parsley and basil.

Opposite: Rosti stacks with spicy peach coulis

WINTER SALADS

WARM PUY LENTIL SALAD

100 g/4 oz puy lentils (dry
weight), cooked
1 bunch spring onions, chopped
6 radishes, halved and sliced
1 orange, segmented
chicory and radicchio leaves to
serve
1 free-range egg, hard-boiled and
finely chopped, to serve
(omit for vegans*)

For the dressing:
1 tablespoon rosemary, finely
chopped
1 teaspoon Dijon mustard
2 tablespoons red wine vinegar
1 tablespoon orange juice
3 tablespoons extra virgin olive oil
zest of ½ orange, finely chopped
pinch of sugar
salt and pepper, to taste

■ Cook the lentils and keep warm. Prepare the spring onions, radishes
and orange and mix into the lentils.
■ Make the dressing and pour over the warm lentils.
■ Arrange the chicory and radicchio leaves around the edge of a serving
platter. Pile the lentils in the centre and sprinkle the finely chopped hard-
boiled egg (omit for vegans*) over the top. Serve immediately.

RED CABBAGE AND ONION SALAD

3 tablespoons olive oil
1 teaspoon cumin seeds
100 g/4 oz red cabbage, shredded
1 red onion, halved and finely sliced
25–50 g/1–2 oz sultanas or
raisins, soaked and drained

1 tablespoon cider vinegar
salt and ground black pepper
1 head Chinese leaves, finely
shredded
6 spring onions, topped and tailed
1 garlic clove, crushed

■ Heat 2 tablespoons of the olive oil in a frying pan and add the cumin
seeds, stirring for a few minutes until they start to colour and pop. Add
the red cabbage and stir-fry for 5 minutes. Remove from the heat and
add the red onion, sultanas or raisins and cider vinegar. Season to taste.
■ Arrange the shredded Chinese leaves around the edge of a platter.
Put the red cabbage in the centre.
■ Heat the remaining olive oil and quickly fry the spring onions and
garlic. Arrange on top of the cabbage and serve.

---

*CAN BE VEGAN

TIP
■
Pick the lentils over very
carefully before soaking
and cooking as they often
contain small pieces of grit.

**SUITABLE FOR
VEGANS**

TIP
■
If the spring onions
are large, cut into
1-cm/½-in pieces on
a slant before cooking,
then scatter over the
red cabbage.

PANETTONE BREAD
AND BUTTER PUDDING

I have never found a vegetarian panettone in the shops, so make my own and use the day-old bread for this recipe. If you prefer not to make your own, this recipe works just as well with any fruit and nut bread. Add extra sultanas to increase the fruity flavour.

1 panettone or other fruit and nut bread, sliced
50 g/2 oz butter
3 free-range eggs
50 g/2 oz caster sugar
2 tablespoons rum or brandy
few drops of vanilla essence
300 ml/½ pint milk
300 ml/½ pint double cream
1 tablespoon demerara sugar
1 teaspoon ground nutmeg

■ Preheat the oven to 180°C/350°F/Gas Mark 4.
■ Grease a shallow ovenproof baking dish. Remove the crusts from the panettone slices. Butter the panettone and arrange the slices in the prepared dish, overlapping each other.
■ Beat together the eggs, caster sugar, rum or brandy and vanilla essence.
■ Heat the milk and cream gently in a saucepan, then bring to the boil. Remove from the heat immediately and pour onto the egg and sugar mixture, stirring all the time.
■ Pour the mixture over the panettone. Mix the demerara sugar and nutmeg together and sprinkle over the top.
■ Stand the dish in a bain-marie (a baking dish half-filled with water) and bake in the preheated oven for 45–50 minutes, until the custard is set and the top is golden.

TIP
■
Bread and butter pudding is a basic but very adaptable dish. Try spreading plain or fruit bread with jam or marmalade before arranging the slices in the dish; or vary the spices and alcohol used, to change the flavours.

WINTER MENU 3

▪

SERVES 4

▪

Chestnut and red wine pâté

Gougère of caramelized vegetables

Roast vegetable purées

Gomasio potatoes

Mango, pineapple and orange fool

SUITABLE FOR VEGANS

CHESTNUT
AND RED WINE PATE

This is a very simple but rich and tasty recipe, which is useful as a sandwich filling as well as a dinner party starter. Buy canned, ready-cooked chestnuts and chestnut purée to make it even easier.

1 tablespoon olive or groundnut oil
1 small onion, finely chopped
1 garlic clove, crushed
pinch of dried thyme
150 ml/¼ pint red wine
150 ml/¼ pint vegetable stock
100 g/4 oz chopped chestnuts
   (cooked weight)
100 g/4 oz chestnut purée

75 g/3 oz wholemeal breadcrumbs
1 tablespoon brandy
2–3 teaspoons shoyu
salt and freshly ground black pepper

To serve:
fresh herbs
crackers
crisp green salad leaves

▪ Heat the oil in a saucepan, and gently cook the onion and garlic with the dried thyme until soft. Add the red wine and vegetable stock and bring to the boil.

▪ Remove from the heat and stir in the chopped chestnuts, chestnut purée, breadcrumbs, brandy and shoyu. Season with salt and pepper to taste. Cook over a gentle heat until thickened.

▪ Spoon the pâté into individual ramekins, smooth the surface and then chill in the refrigerator until required.

▪ Serve garnished with fresh herbs, with crackers and crisp green salad leaves.

GOUGERE OF
CARAMELIZED VEGETABLES

A gougère is simply a ring of choux pastry 'buns'. Other ingredients can be used to fill the centre of the ring. The caramelized root vegetables in this recipe are wonderfully sweet.

4 tablespoons olive oil

6 garlic cloves, peeled and left whole

8 shallots, halved

3 medium carrots, cut into matchsticks

3 medium parsnips, cut into matchsticks

225 g/8 oz sweet potatoes or butternut squash, cut into 1-cm/½-in cubes

pinch of dried basil (or other herb)

1 tablespoon sugar or apple juice concentrate

225 ml/8 fl oz vegetable stock

2 teaspoons tomato purée

salt and freshly ground black pepper

torn fresh basil leaves, to garnish

Choux pastry:

100 g/4 oz plain white flour

pinch of salt

pinch of dried basil (or other herb)

200 ml/7 fl oz water

75 g/3 oz butter

3 free-range eggs, lightly beaten

75 g/3 oz vegetarian Cheddar cheese, grated

> **WINE SUGGESTIONS**
> ■
> **White**
> Opou Riesling
> Millton Vineyard
> *Light, honeyed and medium-dry kiwi white*
>
> **Red**
> Domaine St Michel
> Syrah/Malbec
> *Tasty Midi red with good up-front fruit*

■ Preheat the oven to 220°C/425°F/Gas Mark 7.

■ Sauté the garlic, shallots and carrots in the oil for 5 minutes, until lightly browned. Add the parsnips, sweet potato or squash and dried basil, and sauté for 5 minutes.

■ Add the sugar or apple juice concentrate and stir well. Add the stock and tomato purée, bring to the boil, then reduce the heat and simmer gently until the vegetables are tender. Season and set aside, keeping warm.

■ For the choux pastry, line a greased baking sheet with baking parchment. Mix the flour, salt and dried basil together in a jug. Heat the water and butter gently in a medium-sized saucepan until the butter has melted, and then bring to the boil. Remove from the heat and pour in all the flour at once and beat thoroughly with a wooden spoon. Continue beating over a gentle heat until the flour is incorporated and you have a ball of pastry in the pan.

■ Remove from the heat, cool for 2 minutes, then beat in the eggs, a little at a time. Fold in the cheese and beat well. Spoon the mixture onto the lined baking tray, one tablespoon at a time, to form a ring.

■ Bake in the preheated oven for 20 minutes, until risen and golden. Reduce the temperature to 180°C/350°F/Gas Mark 4 and make small slits in the side of each 'bun' to allow steam to escape. Bake for a further 5 minutes.

■ Transfer the gougère to a serving dish. Reheat the filling and spoon into the centre of the ring. Serve garnished with torn basil leaves.

WINTER
VEGETABLE DISHES

ROAST VEGETABLE PURÉES

Seasonal winter root vegetables are naturally sweet in flavour. As an alternative to mashed potatoes, try making a vegetable purée. Some delicious combinations are:

- Celeriac and ground cumin
- Carrot and ground (or fresh) coriander
- Sweet potato or butternut squash with nutmeg
- Potatoes with saffron and garlic

Boil the vegetable used in the usual way until very tender. Mash with butter or vegan margarine* to taste, then add enough milk or cream (or soya milk* or soya cream*) to give a creamy texture. Add the suggested seasoning and use a piping bag with a large nozzle to pipe a 'nest' or a swirl of the purée on each serving plate, if liked.

GOMASIO POTATOES

The gomasio coating gives the potatoes a distinctive savoury flavour. Just split the cooked potatoes and fill with butter or vegan margarine* to serve.

4 medium-sized baking potatoes
olive oil to coat

For the gomasio:
5 teaspoons sesame seeds
½–1 teaspoon sea salt

- Preheat the oven to 200°C/400°F/Gas Mark 6.
- Scrub the baking potatoes and prick them with a fork. Rub the skins with a little olive oil.
- Dry toast the sesame seeds in a non-stick frying pan until they begin to pop. Put into a grinder with the sea salt and grind until smooth.
- Transfer to a plate and roll the potatoes in the gomasio to coat. Place on a baking tray and cook in the preheated oven for 45–60 minutes, until tender.

MANGO, PINEAPPLE
AND ORANGE FOOL

Exotic fruits are available in the supermarkets all the year round. They brighten up the usual wintry fare of apples, pears and oranges, whereas in the summer they add even more colour to the locally grown soft fruits. Although rich, this dessert is quite light and your guests are bound to come back for more, so there is enough for six helpings!

100 g/4 oz vegetarian trifle sponges
   (or day-old sponge cake)
100 g/4 oz canned pineapple slices
   in fruit juice
1 ripe mango, peeled, stoned and
   sliced (or use canned)
grated rind and juice of 2 oranges
25 g/1 oz sugar

300 ml/10 fl oz double cream
1–2 tablespoons Cointreau
   (optional)

To decorate:
curls of zest and segments of
   2 oranges
sprigs of fresh mint

■ Use the trifle sponges to line the base and halfway up the sides of a glass serving bowl. Drain the pineapple, reserving the juice, and arrange the slices of pineapple and mango over the sponges.

■ Pour 3 tablespoons of the reserved juice over the sponge to moisten. Mix the orange zest and juice with the sugar and stir until completely dissolved.

■ Whip the cream until thick, and then beat in the orange juice and sugar mixture, and the Cointreau, if using.

■ Pour over the fruit and sponge, then cover and chill in the refrigerator for at least 2 hours, until the juices have soaked into the sponge and the cream has thickened.

■ Just before serving, decorate the trifle with orange segments, curls of orange zest and sprigs of mint.

TIP

■

When choosing a mango, check that it is ripe by squeezing it gently in the palm of your hand — it should give slightly. Cut it in half lengthways, feeling down the side of the flat stone with your knife. Once the stone has been removed it can be skinned and sliced quite easily.

PARTY
CANAPES AND FINGER FOOD

Left: Party dips with mixed crudités (page 212), Asparagus and cashew mini tartlets (page 218) and Watermelon and strawberry punch (page 223)

PARTY DIPS
WITH MIXED CRUDITÉS

This is a versatile vegan mayonnaise which can be flavoured with garlic and lemon to make a basic dip, or other ingredients can be added to change the flavour. You could also use the satay sauce from the mushroom satay recipe on page 231 as a party dip.

TIP

∎

Ready-made vegan mayonnaise is now available from health food stores. Plain, or flavoured with lemon or garlic, it can be used as the basis of many different dips.

90 ml/3 fl oz soya milk
juice and zest of ½ lemon
1 garlic clove, crushed
180 ml/6 fl oz cold pressed
   sunflower oil
salt and freshly ground black pepper

Mexican dip:
1 tablespoon chopped coriander
½ avocado, finely chopped
1 tomato, skinned and finely chopped

Curry dip:
1 small onion or shallot
1 tablespoon groundnut oil

1 tablespoon mild curry powder
   or paste
2 tablespoons spicy mango chutney

For the crudités and dippers:
1 red pepper, deseeded and sliced
1 green pepper, deseeded and sliced
1 yellow pepper, deseeded and sliced
3 sticks celery, cut into 5-cm/2-in
   lengths
½ cucumber, cut into thick
   matchsticks
2 carrots, cut into batons
3 pitta breads, cut into triangles
1 packet vegetarian tortilla chips

∎ For each dip, you need one quantity of the basic dip recipe. Place the soya milk, lemon juice and zest and garlic in a blender and blend together briefly. Gradually drizzle in the oil through the feed tube with the motor running until the mixture emulsifies. Season to taste.

∎ If wished, add one of the suggested flavourings. For the Mexican dip, the chopped coriander, avocado and tomato can just be stirred in.

∎ For the curry dip, fry the onion or shallot gently in the oil for 5 minutes, until tender. Add the curry powder or paste and cook for 2 minutes. Stir in the mango chutney. Remove from the heat and cool before stirring into the basic dip.

∎ Serve the dips with a selection of the suggested crudités and dippers.

Each dip serves 6–8

PARTY FOOD TIPS

■ Party food needs to be easy to eat while standing, balancing a plate and a drink in an often crowded room. Finger or fork food is simplest, but try to avoid too many pastry-based dishes. Other useful edible bases are croustades, crostini or vegetable 'boats'.

■ Choose recipes that can be prepared in advance to allow you to enjoy the party too.

■ A selection of hot and cold dishes is good for winter parties. For food that is to be served warm, prepare in advance and reheat in batches.

■ In the summer, lots of dips and crunchy vegetable crudités for dippers are popular.

■ Have a selection of drinks available — red and white wine, beer or lager, perhaps an appropriate punch and some interesting non-alcoholic drinks for those who are driving or prefer to avoid alcohol. If making a punch, make it fruity and not too alcoholic.

■ Many supermarkets and off licences will loan glasses free if you buy your drinks from them; and some will let you have drinks on a sale or return basis — it is better to over- rather than underestimate.

■ Have a plentiful supply of napkins available in case of spills.

■ Make the buffet table as colourful as possible, perhaps following a particular theme. This helps to make the food look even more tempting.

■ Fill gaps on the table with (vegetarian) crisps and snacks.

*Below: Mexican dip
(see opposite)*

OLIVE AND SUN-DRIED
TOMATO PALMIERS

When cold, the palmiers can be stored in an airtight container for 24 hours, then reheated to crisp them up just before serving.

25 g/1 oz strong vegetarian Cheddar cheese, finely grated
25 g/1 oz vegetarian Stilton cheese, finely grated
25 g/1 oz vegetarian Parmesan or Pecorino, finely grated
225 g/8 oz puff pastry (fresh or frozen)
freshly ground black pepper
25 g/1 oz black olives, stoned and finely chopped
25 g/1 oz sun-dried tomatoes, finely chopped

■ Preheat the oven to 220°C/425°F/Gas Mark 7. Mix all the grated cheeses together in a bowl.
■ Roll out the pastry to an oblong strip, 30 × 20 cm/12 × 8 in. Sprinkle the cheese on two-thirds of the pastry, and sprinkle black pepper over the cheese. Bring the pastry end with no cheese up and fold over half the cheese pastry. Fold the remaining cheese pastry third over the rest of the pastry. Press down the edges of the pastry, then roll out again to a square 20 × 20 cm/8 × 8 in. Cut the square in half.
■ On one strip place two-thirds of the chopped olives, and on the other strip put two-thirds of the sun-dried tomatoes, covering the whole strip. For each strip, bring both long edges into the centre so that they meet in the middle. Flatten with a rolling pin and roll out a little.
■ Arrange the remaining one-third of each mixture over the pastry, and fold up again from both long edges to meet in the centre.
■ With a sharp knife, cut into 6-mm/¼-in strips. Place on a greased baking tray, leaving room to expand. Bake in the preheated oven for about 10 minutes, until golden brown. Serve warm.

Makes approx. 24 palmiers

Opposite: Deep-fried fresh vegetable chips (see page 216) and
Olive and sun-dried tomato palmiers

DEEP-FRIED FRESH
VEGETABLE CHIPS

Why buy ready-made, oversalted crisps when you can easily make your own with a variety of vegetables?

juice of 1 lemon
1 large potato
1 sweet potato
1 carrot
1 parsnip

225 g/8 oz celeriac
2 Jerusalem artichokes
1 beetroot
groundnut oil, for deep frying
salt

■ Have a large bowl of iced water ready, into which you have stirred the lemon juice.

■ Peel all the vegetables and slice very thinly. Use a food processor (slicing disk attachment) or a mandolin to make the slices really thin and even. Drop all the vegetable slices, except the beetroot (it will stain all the other vegetables), into the iced lemon water.

■ Drain and dry all the vegetables well on kitchen paper before cooking. Heat the oil in a wok until a cube of bread dropped in rises immediately to the surface and browns in less than a minute. Fry the vegetable slices in batches until crisp. Drain well and sprinkle with salt.

■ These chips can be reheated on a baking sheet in a preheated oven at 220°C/425°F/Gas Mark 7 for a few minutes before serving.

Serves 6

TIP

■

Serve these 'chips' on their own or as crudités to go with the dips on page 212. They can also be served with a main dish at a dinner party and always make an interesting talking point.

CHEESY LEEK AND
SWEET POTATO TORTILLA

Tortillas can be served at any temperature — hot, room temperature or cold, depending on the time of year. This one, which is rather like a pastry-less quiche, makes an excellent supper dish as well as being party food.

225 g/8 oz parsnips, peeled and chopped into small pieces
1 sweet potato, peeled and chopped into small pieces
2 leeks, trimmed, washed and shredded
6 free-range eggs
4 spring onions, finely chopped
salt and freshly ground black pepper
175 g/6 oz vegetarian Stilton, grated or crumbled
25 g/1 oz butter

TIP
■
Try to get an orange sweet potato as this gives extra colour to the dish. Butternut squash also makes a good alternative.

■ Preheat the oven to 180°C/350°F/Gas Mark 4.
■ Cook the parsnips and sweet potato together in boiling water until tender. Drain and cool. Steam the leeks for 3 minutes, then drain and cool.
■ Beat the eggs, then add the sweet potato, parsnips and leeks, the chopped spring onions and seasoning to taste.
■ Butter an ovenproof dish and put half the mixture into it. Sprinkle with the Stilton, then add the rest of the egg mixture.
■ Cover with greased foil and bake in the preheated oven for 40 minutes. Remove the foil and cook for a further 20–30 minutes, until the tortilla feels set and is golden in colour. Cut into wedges and serve with a crisp green salad.

Serves 8

ASPARAGUS AND
CASHEW MINI TARTLETS

TIP

■

The pastry can be
flavoured with a pinch of
dried mixed herbs or, for
a non-vegan version, add
50 g/2 oz grated
vegetarian Cheddar.

Asparagus is in season in early summer and has a very fresh 'green'
flavour. When not in season you could use canned asparagus, but
treat it gently as it tends to be very soft.

225 g/8 oz plain white flour
pinch of salt
100 g/4 oz vegan margarine
4–6 tablespoons cold water
1 tablespoon vegetable oil
1 small onion, finely chopped
100 g/4 oz fresh asparagus tips, steamed until tender
50 g/2 oz cashew nuts, toasted and chopped
1 tablespoon shoyu
salt and freshly ground black pepper
parsley sprigs, to garnish

■ Preheat the oven to 200°C/400°F/Gas Mark 6.
■ Put the flour and salt in a bowl. Rub in the margarine with your fingertips to
resemble breadcrumbs. Mix in enough cold water to make a smooth, firm
dough. Roll into a ball, wrap in cling film and refrigerate for 30 minutes.
■ Heat the oil in a saucepan and fry the onion until golden. Chop the
asparagus and add to the onion with the cashew nuts. Stir in the shoyu, season
to taste with salt and pepper and cool.
■ Roll out the pastry to 2.5 mm/⅛ in thick. Use a pastry cutter to make
twelve 8-cm/3-in circles. Place in a greased patty pan. Prick the surface and
bake 'blind' (filled with baking beans) in the preheated oven for 10 minutes,
until the pastry shells are golden and crisp.
■ Cool on a wire rack. Spoon in
the asparagus and cashew
filling and serve garnished
with parsley sprigs.

Makes 12

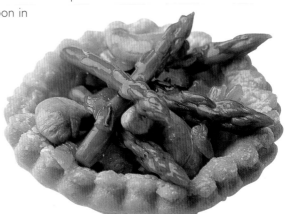

STUFFED
BAKED POTATOES

There are many recipes for baked potato toppings, but removing the cooked flesh, mashing and mixing it with a filling and then reheating the filled shells is more practical for a party as well as being more tasty. As an alternative, use the Crostini toppings on page 174.

6 medium baking potatoes, scrubbed
olive oil, for baking
1 red pepper
50 g/2 oz butter or vegan margarine*
a little milk or soya milk*
100 g/4 oz olives, stoned and chopped
salt and freshly ground black pepper
1 avocado, peeled, stoned and chopped

1 tomato, skinned and chopped
1 tablespoon lemon juice
2 tablespoons chopped fresh
  coriander
1 tablespoon olive oil
100 g/4 oz mushrooms, chopped
1 garlic clove, crushed

- Preheat the oven to 200°C/400°F/Gas Mark 6.
- Rub the baking potatoes with the olive oil and prick all over with a fork. Place on a baking sheet and cook in the preheated oven for 45–60 minutes, until tender when pierced with a knife.
- At the same time, roast the red pepper until the skin is blistered and blackening. Put the pepper into a plastic bag and seal until cool enough to handle. Remove the skin and seeds and chop the flesh.
- Remove the potatoes from the oven, cut in half and spoon the flesh into a bowl. Beat in the butter or vegan margarine* and enough milk or soya milk* to give a creamy texture. Divide between 3 bowls.
- Mix the red pepper with the chopped olives and season to taste. Stir into one of the bowls of potato and use to fill 4 of the potato skin halves.
- Mix the avocado, tomato, lemon juice and coriander and season to taste. Stir into one of the bowls of potato and use to fill 4 of the potato skin halves.
- Heat the olive oil in a saucepan and fry the mushrooms and garlic for a few minutes until tender. Season and stir into the final bowl of potato and use to fill the remaining potato skin halves.
- Reduce the oven temperature to 180°C/350°F/Gas Mark 4, and gently reheat the filled potatoes on a baking tray for about 20–30 minutes. Serve hot.

Serves 12

TIP
■

The juices from the roast peppers are well worth saving and using as part of a salad dressing as they impart a rich, sweet flavour.

FILLED ITALIAN
FOCACCIA BREAD

Focaccia is a delicious Italian bread — the original pizza base. This variation in which the filling is cooked inside the bread makes an excellent party piece!

2 teaspoons sugar	few basil leaves, roughly torn
12 g / ½ oz fresh yeast	4 sun-dried tomatoes in oil, sliced
225 ml/8 fl oz tepid water	I garlic clove, crushed
225 g /8 oz strong white flour	extra olive oil
pinch of salt	12 olives, stoned
2 tablespoons olive oil	2–3 sprigs fresh rosemary
150 g /5 oz mozzarella cheese, sliced	coarse sea salt

■ Preheat the oven to 220°C/425°F/Gas Mark 7.

■ Stir the sugar into the yeast and add a little of the measured tepid water. Leave in a warm place for 5–10 minutes, until bubbles appear on the surface.

■ Mix the flour and salt in a bowl. Pour in the yeast mixture and olive oil. Add enough tepid water, a little at time, to make a pliable but not sticky dough.

■ Knead for 10 minutes on a lightly floured worktop. Leave in an oiled covered bowl in a warm place for about 40–60 minutes, to double in size.

■ Punch the dough down, turn out onto a lightly floured work top and knead for 3 minutes. Halve the dough and roll each half out into a rough circle, about 2.5 mm/⅛ in thick. Grease a baking sheet with olive oil and put one piece of dough onto the oiled surface. Cover with slices of mozzarella cheese, basil leaves and sun-dried tomatoes.

■ Place the second piece of dough over the top. Make some dimples in the top of the focaccia with your fingers.

■ Mix the crushed garlic with some olive oil and brush over the top of the dough. Put some olives in the dimples, then sprinkle with rosemary and sea salt. Leave to prove for 20 minutes.

■ Bake in the preheated oven for 10 minutes. Reduce the oven temperature to 190°C/375°F/Gas Mark 5 and bake for another 15–20 minutes, until golden and evenly cooked. Serve cut into wedges.

LEEK AND MUSHROOM
VOL AU VENTS

*CAN BE VEGAN

Ever popular, these crisp little pastry cups with a tasty leek and mushroom filling are easily made vegan by using soya cream. Make sure that when you take the lids off the cooked pastry cases you remove as much of the pastry inside as possible to leave room for the filling. Fill right to the brim before putting the little hat on.

450 g / 1 lb ready-made vegan puff pastry
1 tablespoon groundnut oil or olive oil
1 large leek, trimmed, washed and finely shredded
100 g / 4 oz mushrooms, finely chopped
2–3 teaspoons shoyu

2.5-cm / 1-in piece fresh ginger root, peeled and grated
salt and freshly ground black pepper
1 tablespoon plain flour
150 ml / 5 fl oz dairy or soya cream*
25 g / 1 oz cashew nuts, toasted and chopped
sprigs of parsley, to garnish

- Preheat the oven to 225°C/450°F/Gas Mark 8.
- Roll out the pastry to 5 mm/¼ in thick and, using a 7.5-cm/3-in pastry cutter, cut out 12 circles. With a 5-cm/2-in cutter, cut an inner circle part way through each (this will form the lid once cooked). Place on a baking sheet and cook in the preheated oven for about 5 minutes, until risen and golden. Cool on a wire rack, then remove the lids and some of the pastry from the centre.

- Heat the oil in a saucepan and gently cook the leek until tender. Add the mushrooms and cook over a high heat to evaporate the liquid. Stir in the shoyu, grated ginger and seasoning.
- Add the flour and cook, stirring, for 2 minutes. Stir in the cream or soya cream* and cook until thickened. Stir in the cashew nuts.
- Reheat the vol au vent cases at 180°C/350°F/Gas Mark 4 for about 15 minutes. Heat the filling and spoon into the hot cases, top with the lids at an angle and pop a sprig of parsley into the sauce. Serve warm.

Makes 12

CREAMY MUSHROOM
CROUSTADES

Use any mushrooms that you like for this recipe — button, field, chestnut, oyster, shiitake — or a mixture. The contrast of the creamy sauce with the crisp base is wonderful.

12 thin slices wholemeal bread, crusts removed
olive oil, for brushing
25 g/1 oz butter or vegan margarine*
1 onion, finely chopped
1 garlic clove, crushed
450 g/1 lb mushrooms, sliced
300 ml/10 fl oz soured cream or soya cream*
salt and freshly ground black pepper
1 teaspoon paprika

■ Preheat the oven to 190°C/375°F/Gas Mark 5.
■ Brush both sides of each slice of bread with olive oil. Place in a jam tart tin, pushing each one down to form a hollow. Bake in the preheated oven for 10–15 minutes, until crisp.
■ Meanwhile, melt the butter or vegan margarine* in a frying pan and fry the onion and garlic until transluscent. Add the mushrooms and continue cooking for a further 5 minutes. Stir in the soured cream or soya cream* and season with salt and pepper.
■ Spoon into the croustade 'nests' and sprinkle with the paprika. Serve the croustades immediately while they are still hot.

Makes 12

TIP
■

Cauliflower cheese would make an alternative topping as would finely diced aubergine quickly fried with red pepper, onion and tomato, then stirred into the cream or soya cream and scattered with chopped fresh herbs.

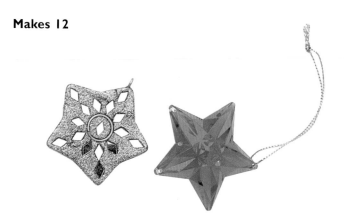

FESTIVE PARTY PUNCH

2 litres/3¼ pints vegetarian red
   wine
1 orange, sliced
1 lemon, sliced
100 g/4 oz sugar
1 piece cinnamon stick
6 whole cloves
1 piece dried ginger, bruised

½ tablespoon allspice berries
Cointreau (optional)

To garnish:
1 orange, sliced
1 lemon, sliced
2 apples, sliced
few sprigs of mint

■ Put all the ingredients (except the Cointreau, if using) into a large pan. Bring
to the boil, then remove from the heat and leave to stand for 2 hours.
■ Put ½ tablespoon of Cointreau in each serving glass, if using. Reheat the
punch, almost to boiling point, and transfer to a punch bowl. Garnish with
fresh fruit slices and sprigs of mint.
■ Pour into the glasses over the liqueur when the punch has cooled slightly.

Serves 12

WATERMELON AND
STRAWBERRY PUNCH

1 watermelon
225 g/8 oz fresh strawberries,
   washed
crushed ice
2 bottles sparkling or dry white
   wine, chilled

1 bottle soda water, chilled

To garnish:
melon balls
strawberry halves
mint leaves

■ Peel and deseed the watermelon and hull the strawberries. Purée half of
the fruit in a liquidizer or food processor, then press through a sieve.
■ Transfer to a punch bowl with some of the crushed ice and add the
wine and soda water.
■ Make melon balls with a Parisienne baller and cut the reserved
strawberries in half. Add to the bowl with the mint leaves. Put the
remaining crushed ice in each wine glass as you serve the punch.

Serves 12–16

DINNER
PARTIES

Left: Paneer or tofu and vegetable moghlai (page 236) and Spicy vegetable filo samosas (page 235)

**SUMMER
MENU**

▪

SERVES 4

▪

Fresh pea and mint
soup with croûtons

Almond, coriander
and cheese tuiles

Meringue stacks
filled with summer
fruits

*CAN BE VEGAN

FRESH PEA AND MINT
SOUP WITH CROUTONS

The flavour of fresh garden peas conjures up long summer days
and sunshine. If you are unable to obtain fresh peas or find
shelling them too much trouble, then use frozen ones instead.

25 g/1 oz butter or vegan margarine*
1 onion, finely chopped
225 g/8 oz leeks, finely shredded and
washed, keeping as much of the
dark green as possible
225 g/8 oz potatoes, peeled and cut
into small chunks
1.2 litres/2 pints light vegetable
stock (use vegan bouillon powder)
225 g/8 oz fresh or frozen peas
(weight without pod)

1 small bunch of mint, chopped
salt and freshly ground black pepper
single cream or soya cream*
mint sprigs, to garnish

Croûtons:
2 slices white bread
2 tablespoons olive oil
1 tablespoon chopped mint

■ Melt the butter or vegan margarine* in a saucepan and gently fry the onion
until soft. Add the leeks and cook for a further 5 minutes.

■ Add the potatoes and stock, bring to the boil, then simmer, covered, for
about 20 minutes, until the potatoes are tender. Add the peas and mint and
simmer for a further 5 minutes.

■ Allow the soup to cool, then liquidize in a blender or food processor until
very smooth. Return to a clean saucepan, reheat gently and season to taste
with salt and pepper.

■ Serve the soup garnished with a swirl of single cream or soya cream*, a
mint sprig and croûtons.　.

■ For the croûtons: mix the mint and olive oil together and season. Brush
the bread on both sides with the oil and bake in a preheated oven at
200°C/400°F/Gas Mark 6 for 10–15 minutes, until crisp. Remove the crusts
and cut into cubes.

Opposite: Fresh pea and mint soup with croûtons

ALMOND, CORIANDER
AND CHEESE TUILES

**WINE
SUGGESTIONS**
■

White
Domaine Spiropoulos
Orino
*Clean and headily
aromatic Greek wine*

Red
Beaujolais Supérieur
Château Boisfranc
Light, fruity and accessible

Tuiles are usually associated with desserts, filled with cream and fruit, but these savoury ones make a lovely alternative to a pastry base for holding grilled vegetables.

25 g/1 oz butter
25 g/1 oz plain white flour
½ teaspoon ground coriander
15 g/½ oz ground almonds
salt and freshly ground black
  pepper
2 free-range egg whites
25 g/1 oz vegetarian Parmesan or
  Pecorino, grated
fresh coriander and lemon zest

Artichoke filling:
450 g/1 lb can of artichokes, drained
2 red peppers
12 Kalamata olives, stoned and halved
1 tablespoon chopped fresh coriander
salt and freshly ground black pepper

Herb sauce:
150 ml/5 fl oz soured cream
juice of ½ lemon
25 g/1 oz fresh coriander, chopped

■ Preheat the oven to 220°C/425°F/Gas Mark 7.

■ Melt the butter in a small saucepan. Sift the flour and ground coriander into a bowl. Mix in the ground almonds and season with salt and pepper.

■ Pour the melted butter and egg whites into the bowl and mix all the ingredients together with an electric hand mixer until you have a light batter.

■ Line a baking sheet with non-stick baking parchment. To make 2 tuiles, spoon 2 tablespoons of batter per portion onto the tray, spacing them well apart.

■ Smooth each spoonful out to a circle, about 15 cm/6 in diameter. Sprinkle with grated cheese and bake for 4 minutes in the preheated oven.

■ Remove the tray from the oven and immediately mould each biscuit over the base of a greased dariole mould to make a little basket (tuile). Replace the biscuits, still on their moulds, in the oven for 5–6 minutes and then unmould and cool. Repeat the process to make 4 tuiles in total.

■ For the filling: quarter the artichokes and grill until charred. Quarter the red peppers and grill, skin side up, until starting to blacken. Cool then remove the skin and seeds and chop. Mix together the peppers, artichokes, olives, coriander and seasoning.

■ Mix all the sauce ingredients or, for a greener sauce, whizz together in a blender.

■ Place a tuile on each serving plate. Fill with the artichoke mixture and drizzle a little of the sauce over the vegetables and onto the plate around the tuile. Garnish with fresh coriander leaves and lemon zest.

Opposite: Almond, coriander and cheese tuiles

MERINGUE STACKS
FILLED WITH SUMMER FRUITS

You can use any combination of soft fruits with these meringues; to get the best flavours, opt for whatever is in season.

2 free-range egg whites
100 g / 4 oz caster sugar
sunflower or groundnut oil, for brushing
300 ml / 10 fl oz double or whipping cream
1 tablespoon Cointreau (or to taste)
225 g / 8 oz mixed summer fruits, e.g. strawberries, black grapes, peaches, kiwis, redcurrants

To garnish:
fanned strawberries
redcurrants
icing sugar, for dusting

■ Preheat the oven to 130°C/250°F/Gas Mark ½.
■ Whisk the egg whites in a grease-free bowl until stiff and dry. Whisk in half of the caster sugar, then fold in the remainder with a metal spoon.
■ Draw eight 10-cm/4-in diameter circles on a sheet of baking parchment, place on a baking tray and brush each circle with a little oil. Divide the meringue evenly between the 8 circles and spread smoothly with a spatula.
■ Bake in the preheated oven for 2 hours, until the meringue has dried out but without colouring. Remove from the tray and cool on a wire rack.
■ Whip the cream until firm and then beat in the Cointreau. Wash and dry the fruit, slicing if necessary.
■ Place 4 meringue circles on serving plates, spread evenly with the cream and arrange a mixture of the fruit on top. Cover with a second meringue circle, securing it in place with a little blob of cream in the centre. Arrange more fruit decoratively on top.
■ Decorate the plate around each meringue stack with fanned strawberries and redcurrants. Dust with a little icing sugar and serve.

TIP
■

Try adding a few drops of vegetarian red food colouring to the egg whites with the sugar. This colours the meringue pink on the inside and makes a lovely contrast to the white of the outside and the cream, complementing the vivid colouring of the fruit.

SPICED MUSHROOM SATAY

Many recipes for satay sauce use peanut butter as a short cut. The flavour of the sauce is better, however, if whole, ready-roasted, unsalted peanuts are used and ground finely in a coffee grinder attachment.

225 g/8 oz fresh shiitake mushrooms (or soaked, dried mushrooms)
3 tablespoons chilli or garlic flavoured oil
4 slices wholemeal bread, toasted, cut into triangles and crusts removed

Satay sauce:
2 tablespoons groundnut oil
1 shallot, finely chopped
2 garlic cloves, crushed
2 large red chillies, deseeded and chopped
1 teaspoon grated fresh root ginger
1 tablespoon very finely chopped lemon grass
1/2 teaspoon salt
100 g/4 oz plain roasted peanuts, finely ground
200 ml/7 fl oz coconut milk
2 tablespoons dark muscovado sugar
1 tablespoon lime juice
freshly ground black pepper

∎ Make the sauce: heat the groundnut oil in a saucepan and fry the shallot and garlic until starting to colour. Add the chillies, ginger, lemon grass and salt and cook for 2–3 minutes.

∎ Add the peanuts, stir well to mix, then add the coconut milk and sugar. Bring to the boil and then simmer gently until the sauce thickens. Season with lime juice and black pepper and keep warm.

∎ Remove the stalks from the mushrooms and cut each mushroom into quarters. Thread onto 4 soaked 15-cm/6-in long wooden skewers, brush well with the chilli or garlic oil and grill gently until cooked through.

∎ Drizzle the satay sauce over the mushroom kebabs and serve hot with triangles of wholemeal toast.

THAI VEGETABLE
CURRY WITH FRAGRANT RICE

Lemon grass, coriander, chillies, coconut milk — all these flavours belong to the wonderful food of Thailand. This curry is based on the traditional Thai green curry found in many restaurants.

WINE SUGGESTIONS

■

White
Gewürztraminer
Pierre Frick
An aromatic bouquet and delightfully spicy flavour

Red
Dominio los Piños Tinto
Warm and supple Spanish red

225 g/8 oz Thai fragrant rice
grated lime zest
1 tablespoon chopped fresh
  lemon grass
1 garlic clove, crushed
½ bunch Thai basil
½ bunch fresh coriander, chopped
1–2 small (hot) red chillies, deseeded
  and finely chopped
4–5 tablespoons water
½ teaspoon black peppercorns
2 tablespoons groundnut oil
100 g/4 oz shallots or red onions,
  halved and sliced

1 garlic clove, crushed
1 small aubergine, cut into
  1-cm/½-in cubes
1 courgette, cut into
  1-cm/½-in cubes
100 g/4 oz green beans, cut into
  2.5-cm/1-in slices
100 g/4 oz mange tout, topped and
  tailed
300 ml/½ pint coconut milk
juice of ½ lime or lemon
salt and freshly ground black pepper
Thai basil and fresh coriander, to
  garnish

■ Cook the rice according to the instructions on the packet. Drain well, stir in the lime zest and keep warm.

■ Meanwhile, blend the lemon grass, garlic, basil, coriander, chillies, water and black peppercorns to a paste.

■ Heat the oil in a saucepan and gently fry the shallots or onions, garlic and aubergine for 5 minutes. Add the aromatic paste and cook over a gentle heat for 2 minutes.

■ Add the other vegetables and coconut milk and simmer for 15–20 minutes, until cooked. Add the lime or lemon juice, salt and pepper.

■ Serve the curry with the Thai fragrant rice, garnished with sprigs of Thai basil and fresh coriander.

Opposite: Thai vegetable curry with fragrant rice

JAPANESE GREEN
TEA ICE CREAM

Japanese green tea powder is used to flavour this unusual and delicious ice cream. Serve with seasonal and colourful fruits to make a visual contrast to the bright green of the ice cream. Green tea powder can be purchased in Asian and Oriental food stores.

1½ tablespoons green tea powder
100 g/4 oz caster sugar
300 ml/½ pint milk
4 free-range egg yolks
1½ tablespoons cornflour
few drops of vanilla essence
225 ml/8 fl oz whipping cream
raspberries and redcurrants, to serve

■ Mix the green tea powder and 1 tablespoon of the caster sugar together in a bowl.

■ Gently heat the milk in a saucepan to blood heat, then pour gradually onto the green tea powder, stirring all the time. Sieve to remove any lumps.

■ Beat the egg yolks and remaining sugar together until pale and creamy. Stir into the green tea mixture. Sift the cornflour over the liquid and fold in gently with the vanilla essence.

■ Return to the saucepan and heat gently, stirring with a wooden spoon, until thick and creamy. Cool.

■ Whip the cream to the soft peak stage, then fold into the mixture. Either churn in an ice cream machine, following the manufacturer's instructions, or turn into a metal bowl and freeze for about 3–4 hours, whisking the partially frozen ice cream twice during this time.

■ Serve the ice cream, decorated with raspberries and redcurrants or other fruit of your choice.

TIP

■

Japanese food always looks wonderful served on black china. The raspberries or redcurrants can be 'frosted' by dipping into a little egg white and then into caster sugar.

SPICY VEGETABLE
FILO SAMOSAS

Use left-over potatoes and other vegetables to vary the filling in these mildly spicy samosas. Samosas can be eaten as a snack food too and are good for a buffet dish at any time of the year.

1 tablespoon groundnut oil
1 onion, finely chopped
2 garlic cloves, crushed
1 green chilli, deseeded and chopped
2.5-cm/1-in piece of fresh root ginger, peeled and grated
1 teaspoon cumin seeds
1 teaspoon ground coriander
1/2 teaspoon turmeric
3 tablespoons chopped fresh coriander

pinch of salt
juice of 1/2 lemon
100 g/4 oz potatoes, finely chopped and steamed
200 g/7 oz can of processed peas, drained
1 packet filo pastry
25 g/1 oz butter or vegan margarine*, melted
selection of chutneys and raitas, to serve

- Preheat the oven to 190°C/375°F/Gas Mark 5.
- Heat the oil in a frying pan and fry the onion and garlic until soft. Add the chilli, ginger, spices, fresh coriander, salt and lemon juice. Stir well to mix. Add the cooked potatoes and peas. Mix well and leave to cool.
- Cut the filo sheets into 9 × 30-cm/4 × 12-in strips. Use 2 strips at a time, keeping the rest covered with a clean damp cloth.
- Brush one strip lightly with melted butter or vegan margarine* and place the second strip on top. Brush again. Place 1 1/2 tablespoons of the samosa mixture at one end of the strip.
- Fold the end of the pastry over the filling, making a triangular shape, and continue folding up the strip to the top, alternating diagonal and straight folds to maintain the triangular shape. Repeat with the rest of the pastry and mixture until all of it is used up.
- Brush the samosas with melted butter or vegan margarine*. Place on an oiled baking sheet and bake in the preheated oven for about 20 minutes, until crisp and golden.
- Serve the samosas with mango chutney, lime pickle and cucumber raita (yogurt mixed with chopped cucumber and fresh mint).

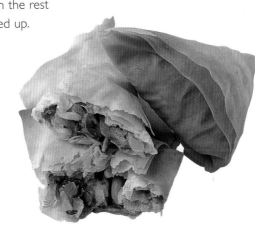

PANEER OR TOFU
AND VEGETABLE MOGHLAI

DRINKS TIP
■

Spicy aromatic white wines, especially Gewürztraminer from Alsace, Irsai Oliver from Hungary and fruity dry Muscats, complement Indian food. Alternatively, a good-quality premium lager may be preferred.

Rich, creamy and delicately spicy are the attributes that characterize this style of cooking. Paneer is an Indian cheese which is stocked by many supermarkets and is similar in texture to a firm block of tofu; both keep their shape and texture when cooked.

2.5-cm/1-in piece fresh root ginger, peeled and grated
4 garlic cloves, crushed
50 g/2 oz ground almonds
6–8 tablespoons water
2 tablespoons groundnut oil
225 g/8 oz paneer or plain tofu*, cut into 2.5-cm/1-in pieces
10 whole cardamom pods
2.5-cm/1-in stick cinnamon
6 whole cloves
1 tablespoon whole coriander seeds
2 teaspoons whole cumin seeds

1 onion, finely chopped
1 green chilli, deseeded and finely chopped
100 g/4 oz green beans, sliced into 2.5-cm/1-in pieces
1 courgette, sliced
300 ml/10 fl oz single cream or soya cream*
50 g/2 oz sultanas
salt, to taste
25 g/1 oz toasted flaked almonds, to garnish

■ In a bowl, blend the ginger, garlic, ground almonds and water together to make a smooth paste.

■ Heat the oil in a frying pan and gently cook the paneer or tofu* until golden on both sides. Drain on kitchen paper and set aside.

■ Put the whole spices into the same oil and cook for 2 minutes. Add the onion and chilli and cook until golden. Add the ginger paste, green beans and courgette and cook for a further 2 minutes.

■ Stir in the cream and paneer or tofu* and soya cream* and simmer for 10–15 minutes, until the vegetables are cooked. Stir in the sultanas. Add salt to taste.

■ Garnish with toasted almonds and serve with boiled rice.

KULFI

The Indian equivalent of ice cream, this is a very refreshing dessert to serve after a spicy meal. The flavours can be complemented by serving cardamom tea or coffee at the end of the meal.

900 ml/1 ½ pints full-cream milk
4 whole cardamom pods
75 g/3 oz soft brown sugar
25 g/1 oz ground almonds
150 ml/5 fl oz double cream
25 g/1 oz pistachio nuts, chopped
chopped pistachio nuts, to decorate

■ Place the milk and cardamom pods in a heavy-based saucepan and bring to the boil. Lower the heat and simmer gently for about 1 hour, until the milk has reduced in volume by half.

■ Add the sugar, stirring until dissolved, then strain into a bowl and add the ground almonds. Leave to cool. Stir the double cream and pistachios into the cold mixture.

■ Use an ice cream maker (following the manufacturer's instructions) or freeze in a metal bowl until mushy. Beat with an electric hand whisk and then freeze again until solid.

■ Transfer the kulfi to the refrigerator 30 minutes before serving. Scoop out and serve decorated with chopped pistachio nuts.

Right: Paneer or tofu and vegetable moghlai

CREAM CHEESE AND HERB PATE

This is a very simple pâté to prepare. It can be made in advance and kept in the refrigerator for 24 hours before your dinner party. You can use other herbs or nuts — in fact, any combination that you fancy. This pâté makes a good sandwich filling too or can be used for filling sticks of celery, quarters of pepper or cherry tomato halves for finger buffets.

225 g /8 oz cream cheese (for low-fat version use Quark)
50 g/2 oz walnuts, ground
1 tablespoon chopped fresh flat-leaf parsley
1 tablespoon chopped fresh chives
1 tablespoon chopped fresh tarragon
pinch of chilli powder
salt and freshly ground black pepper

To serve:
4 walnut halves
sprigs of herbs and chive flowers
pinch of paprika
melba toast

■ Beat the cream cheese in a bowl until it is smooth. Stir in all the other ingredients thoroughly and season to taste.
■ Spoon the pâté mixture into 4 individual ramekins, pressing down firmly. Refrigerate until required.
■ Garnish the top of each ramekin with a walnut half. Place each ramekin on a serving plate and decorate the plates with sprigs of herbs, chive flowers and a sprinkling of paprika. Serve with melba toast.

HAZELNUT AND HERB
TARTS FILLED WITH MUSHROOMS

Individual tarts are more appealing for a special occasion than cutting slices from a large one. These tarts look lovely presented on a white plate in a circle of colourful mixed salad leaves with a drizzle of lemony vinaigrette.

200 g/7 oz plain flour
pinch of salt
100 g/4 oz butter, cubed
50 g/2 oz hazelnuts, chopped and roasted
1 tablespoon chopped fresh thyme or rosemary
1 free-range egg yolk
2–3 tablespoons iced water

Mushroom filling:
225 g/8 oz shallots, quartered
2 tablespoons groundnut oil
1 tablespoon soft brown sugar

2 garlic cloves, crushed
225 g/8 oz exotic mushrooms, e.g. mixed oyster, shiitake, field and straw mushrooms, sliced fairly thickly
300 ml/10 fl oz crème fraîche
1 tablespoon chopped fresh thyme or rosemary
salt and freshly ground black pepper

To garnish:
sliced button mushrooms
pinch of paprika
chopped fresh parsley

WINE SUGGESTIONS
■
White
Domaine St Michel Chardonnay
Full fruited, crisp dry white

Red
Domaine Cabrairal Corbières
Fairly robust and well balanced Midi red

■ Preheat the oven to 200°C/400°F/Gas Mark 6.
■ Sift the flour and salt into a bowl. Cut the butter into small pieces and rub in until the mixture resembles breadcrumbs. Stir in the hazelnuts and herbs and mix with the egg yolk and iced water to make a smooth dough. Knead briefly, then wrap in cling film and refrigerate for 30 minutes.
■ Cook the shallots gently in the oil for about 10 minutes. Stir in the sugar and garlic and continue cooking until the shallots are golden and soft. Add the mushrooms and cook for 5 minutes, stirring all the time. Take off the heat, cool and add the crème fraîche, herbs and seasoning.
■ Roll out the pastry and cut to fit 4 individual 10-cm/4-in loose-bottomed flan tins. Prick the bases and refrigerate for 30 minutes.
■ Bake the pastry cases 'blind' (filled with baking beans) for 15 minutes in the preheated oven. Reduce the heat to 180°C/350°F/Gas Mark 4. Fill with the mushroom mixture and bake for 15 minutes.
■ Turn the tarts out of the tins and garnish with a sliced button mushroom, a sprinkling of paprika and some chopped parsley.

APRICOT AND PECAN
PUDDINGS WITH TOFFEE SAUCE

TIP

■

Pear and hazelnut or plum and almond are also delicious combinations which can be substituted in these puddings. Use almond essence in place of vanilla to intensify the nutty flavour.

There is a great combination of textures in these very light puddings, which are served with a delicious toffee sauce.

50 g / 2 oz light muscovado sugar
50 g / 2 oz pecan nuts, chopped
100 g / 4 oz ready-to-eat dried
   apricots, chopped
pecan nut halves, to garnish

Almond base:
75 g / 3 oz butter or vegan margarine*
60 ml / 2 fl oz maple syrup or soft
   brown sugar
1 free-range egg, beaten or
   1 tablespoon soya flour mixed
   with 2 tablespoons water*

75 g / 3 oz ground almonds
25 g / 1 oz soya flour
½ teaspoon baking powder
few drops of vanilla essence

Toffee sauce:
200 g / 7 oz light muscovado sugar
90 ml / 3 fl oz double cream or soya
   cream*
100 g / 4 oz unsalted butter or vegan
   margarine*
½ teaspoon vanilla essence
25 g / 1 oz chopped pecan nuts

■ Preheat the oven to 180°C/350°F/Gas Mark 4.

■ To make the topping, mix the sugar, chopped pecans and dried apricots together. Divide equally between 4 well-greased, individual ramekins.

■ Cream the butter or margarine* for the base with the maple syrup or sugar. Add the egg or soya flour paste* and mix well. Stir in the almonds, soya flour, baking powder and vanilla essence.

■ Spoon the mixture into the ramekins, place on a baking tray and bake in the preheated oven for 20–30 minutes

■ Make the sauce: put the sugar in a saucepan and use a wooden spoon to crush any lumps. Add the cream and butter (or soya cream* and vegan margarine*) and stir together over a gentle heat until the butter has melted. Bring to the boil and simmer for 2–3 minutes, until toffee-coloured. Remove from the heat, then stir in the vanilla essence and chopped pecans.

■ Turn each pudding out onto a serving plate. Decorate with pecan halves. Spoon a little toffee sauce around the puddings and serve immediately.

Opposite: Apricot and pecan pudding with toffee sauce

DESSERTS

*Left: Chocolate espresso and roasted pecan tarte (page 263)
and Lemon curd profiteroles (page 249)*

PEAR AND STEM
GINGER SORBET

Ginger comes in many forms: fresh root, pickled, ground and preserved in syrup. All are delicious and there is no better combination than pear and ginger.

675 g/1½ lb pears, peeled, cored and sliced
450 ml/15 fl oz water
175 g/6 oz caster sugar
1 tablespoon lemon juice
2 pieces stem ginger in syrup, finely chopped
1 tablespoon stem ginger syrup
mint sprigs, to garnish
strawberry halves, to garnish

■ Stew the pears in the water until soft. Drain the pears, reserving the liquid, and purée the fruit.
■ Fast boil the reserved liquid to reduce it to 300 ml/½ pint. Stir in the sugar until dissolved, bring to the boil and boil for 3–4 minutes to make a sugar syrup.
■ Add all the other ingredients and pour into a polythene or metal container.
■ Cool, then freeze uncovered until half frozen. Mash the mixture well to break up any icy particles and return to the freezer until solid. Alternatively, use an ice cream maker (following the manufacturer's instructions).
■ Remove from the freezer 10–20 minutes before serving, mashing with a fork to break up the crystals. Shape the sorbet between 2 spoons or use a scoop and place in sundae dishes. Garnish with mint sprigs and strawberry halves.

Serves 4

TIP
■
Sorbets are very refreshing at the end of a summer meal. This one is lovely served with Florentines (see page 261).

SPICY TOFFEE APPLE
ICE CREAM

Toffee apples are a traditional part of Hallowe'en. This recipe is a way in which adults can indulge in these sweet flavours without the stickiness of an apple covered in toffee. Why wait for Hallowe'en anyway — this dish is good to serve all year round.

300 ml/½ pint full cream milk
300 ml/10 fl oz double cream
1 vanilla pod, split lengthways
6 medium free-range egg yolks
175 g/6 oz caster sugar
450 g/1 lb dessert apples, peeled, cored and chopped
2 tablespoons lemon juice

½–1 teaspoon ground cinnamon or mixed spice (optional)
75 g/3 oz vegetarian toffees, cut into pieces

To garnish:
mint leaves
lemon zest curls

■ Put the milk, cream and vanilla pod in a saucepan and bring to the boil. Remove from the heat and leave the flavours to infuse for 15 minutes. Strain and discard the vanilla pod and seeds.

■ Whisk the egg yolks and sugar together in a bowl until pale and fluffy. Then whisk in the vanilla cream and pour the mixture into a clean saucepan. Cook over a very low heat, stirring all the time, until the mixture thickens and coats the back of a wooden spoon. Remove from the heat and allow to cool.

■ Place the prepared apples in a saucepan with the lemon juice and cook over a low heat until soft. Mash and leave to cool. Stir in the spices, if using.

■ Stir the toffee pieces and apples into the custard and pour into a shallow polythene container. Freeze for 30 minutes, then beat with a fork. Repeat this process, then freeze until hard (alternatively, use an ice cream making machine, following the manufacturer's instructions).

■ Take out of the freezer for 30 minutes before serving. Scoop into sundae dishes and decorate with mint leaves and lemon zest curls.

Serves 4

LEMON CURD
ICE CREAM

To make a quicker ice cream that does not need beating during the freezing process, use 450 ml / ¾ pint each of whipped double cream and Greek yogurt. Fold together with 175 g / 6 oz icing sugar and a few drops of vanilla essence. Fold in the lemon curd and turn into a polythene container and freeze until solid.

300 ml / ½ pint full-cream milk
300 ml / ½ pint double cream
1 vanilla pod, split lengthways
6 medium free-range egg yolks
175 g / 6 oz caster sugar
mint leaves and lemon zest curls,
    to garnish

For the lemon curd:
juice and grated zest of 1 lemon
1 large free-range egg
35 g / 1 ½ oz caster sugar
25 g / 1 oz unsalted butter, cut into
    small pieces

■ Make the lemon curd first. Whisk the lemon juice and egg together in a bowl.

■ In a separate bowl, mix together the lemon zest and sugar. Pour the whisked egg over the sugar and add the butter.

■ Place the bowl over a pan of simmering water, stirring frequently with a wooden spoon until thick. Leave to cool.

■ Make the ice cream. Put the milk, cream and vanilla pod into a saucepan and bring to the boil. Remove from the heat and leave the flavours to infuse for 15 minutes. Strain and discard the vanilla pod and seeds.

■ Whisk the egg yolks and sugar together in a bowl until pale and fluffy. Then whisk in the vanilla cream and pour the mixture into a clean saucepan.

■ Cook over a very low heat, stirring all the time, until the mixture thickens and coats the back of a wooden spoon. Remove from the heat and allow to cool.

■ Stir the lemon curd into the custard and pour into a shallow polythene container. Freeze for 30 minutes, then beat with a fork. Repeat this process, then freeze until hard (alternatively, use an ice cream making machine, following the manufacturer's instructions).

■ Take the ice cream out of the freezer for 30 minutes before serving. Scoop into sundae dishes and decorate with mint leaves and lemon zest curls.

Serves 4

Opposite: Lemon curd ice cream

SHORTBREAD TARTS
WITH FRESH FRUIT

This is a very summery dessert and would be a lovely finish to an *al fresco* meal. Assemble the tarts just before serving to prevent the pastry becoming soggy.

TIP

■

Substitute 50 g/2 oz finely ground roasted hazelnuts for 50 g/2 oz of the plain flour to give the pastry a nutty flavour.

100 g/4 oz butter or vegan margarine*
175 g/6 oz white flour
50 g/2 oz soft brown muscovado sugar
1–2 tablespoons milk or soya milk*
100 g/4 oz strawberries, sliced
2 kiwi fruit, sliced
100 g/4 oz blueberries
icing sugar and mint leaves, to decorate

Crème patissière:
300 ml/½ pint soya milk
1 vanilla pod
2 heaped tablespoons vegan custard powder
2 tablespoons caster sugar
½ teaspoon vanilla essence
100 ml/4 fl oz soya cream

■ Preheat the oven to 150°C/300°F/Gas Mark 2.
■ Rub the butter or vegan margarine* into the flour until it resembles breadcrumbs. Add the sugar and mix well. Work the mixture together to form a firm dough, adding a little milk or soya milk* if necessary. Press into 4 individual (or one 20-cm/8-in) flan ring(s), moulding the dough up the sides. Bake in the preheated oven for about 35–45 minutes. Cool, then turn out onto a serving dish.
■ To make the crème patissière, heat the soya milk to boiling point in a saucepan. Add a vanilla pod, turn off the heat and set aside for 30 minutes. Place the custard powder and caster sugar in a bowl. Mix to a paste with a little of the soya milk.
■ Remove the vanilla pod from the remaining soya milk, and return to the boil. Pour onto the custard powder paste, stir well and return to the pan. Bring to the boil, stirring continuously. Reduce the heat to a simmer and cook for a further 2 minutes, until it thickens. Remove from the heat, stir in the vanilla essence and soya cream. Cool completely.
■ Spoon the crème patissière into the shortbread cases. Decorate with the prepared fruit. Dust with icing sugar and decorate with sprigs of mint.

Serves 4

LEMON CURD
PROFITEROLES

I always make my own lemon curd as most of the ready-made ones contain battery eggs — it also tastes better and is quite quick and easy, which is just as well as a batch never lasts very long.

150 ml/¼ pint water
50 g/2 oz butter
pinch of salt
65 g/2½ oz plain white flour (in a jug)
2 large free-range eggs, beaten
100 g/4 oz icing sugar, sifted
juice of ½–1 lemon
150 ml/5 fl oz single or double cream

Lemon curd:
zest and juice of 2 lemons
2 large free-range eggs
75 g/3 oz caster sugar
50 g/2 oz unsalted
   butter cut into
   small pieces

■ Preheat the oven to 220°C/425°F/Gas Mark 7.
■ Make the lemon curd first. Whisk the lemon juice and eggs together in a bowl. In a separate bowl, mix together the lemon zest and sugar. Pour the eggs over the sugar and add the butter. Place over a pan of simmering water, stirring frequently with a wooden spoon, until thick. Leave to cool.
■ Put the water, butter and salt for the choux pastry in a saucepan and heat until the water is just boiling and the butter has melted.
■ Remove from the heat and add all the flour at once by pouring it from the jug. Beat to form a shiny dough, then return to the heat and cook for 2 minutes, stirring frequently until you have a ball of dough in the centre of the pan.
■ Add the beaten egg, a little at a time, beating well between each addition. You should have a glossy dough of piping consistency. The more you beat at this stage, the lighter and crisper the pastry will be.
■ Either spoon the choux pastry onto a parchment-lined baking sheet, a tablespoon at a time, or put the mixture into a piping bag with a large nozzle and pipe 'blobs'. Bake in the preheated oven for 15 minutes, then reduce the heat to 190°C/375°F/Gas Mark 5 for a further 10–15 minutes, until crisp and golden.
■ Remove from the oven, and slit each profiterole to allow the steam to escape. Cool on a wire rack, then fill with lemon curd.
■ Mix the icing sugar and lemon juice to make a thin glacé icing.
Pile the profiteroles up on a dish and drizzle the lemon icing over the top. Serve with cream.

Serves 4 (makes 12 profiteroles)

NECTARINE AND
PHYSALIS CREAM PIE

Fresh nectarines are only available for a short season. You can substitute other fruit in this pie — pears work especially well if you use almond essence in place of vanilla in the custard cream.

50 g / 2 oz butter
100 g / 4 oz plain white flour
2 teaspoons soft brown sugar
2–3 tablespoons chilled water
4–6 physalis, opened out to expose the fruit, to garnish

Fruit filling:
300 ml / ½ pint milk
2 free-range egg yolks, lightly beaten
2 teaspoons sugar

few drops of vanilla essence
grated zest of ½ lemon
2 teaspoons plain white flour
3 tablespoons extra thick double cream
4 ripe nectarines, stoned and sliced
100 g / 4 oz physalis halved

Meringue topping:
2 free-range egg whites
100 g / 4 oz caster sugar

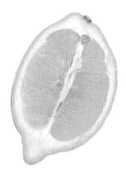

■ Preheat the oven to 200°C/400°F/Gas Mark 6.

■ Rub the butter into the flour to resemble breadcrumbs. Stir in the sugar and mix to a dough with chilled water. Roll into a ball, wrap in cling film and refrigerate for 30 minutes.

■ Roll out the dough to fit a 20-cm/8-in flan ring, then bake 'blind' (filled with baking beans) for 5–10 minutes. Remove from the oven and reduce the heat to 120°C/250°F/Gas Mark ½.

■ Make the filling. Bring the milk to the boil. In a bowl, mix the egg yolks, sugar, vanilla essence, lemon zest and flour. Pour the boiled milk into the bowl and mix well. Return to the saucepan and heat gently, stirring, until thickened. When cool, stir in the double cream.

■ Pour the custard into the part-cooked flan case. Arrange slices of nectarine and halved physalis on top.

■ Whip the egg whites in a grease-free bowl, then add the sugar, a tablespoon at a time, whisking until you have a meringue. Spread over the top of the flan.

■ Place on a baking tray and bake gently for about 1 hour.

■ Allow to go cold, then place the pie overnight (about 8 hours) in the refrigerator, so that the filling becomes firm. Serve decorated with the extra physalis.

Serves 4–6

FRESH SUMMER
FRUIT BRULEE

This dish can be prepared in advance and the sugar on the topping caramelized just before serving. Ideal as the finish to an *al fresco* meal, the sugar will still be bubbling as you carry it into the garden. The vegan topping makes a delicious alternative to the more traditional dairy version.

100 g/4 oz strawberries, halved
50 g/2 oz seedless green grapes, halved
½ melon, flesh scooped out into balls
2 ripe peaches, stoned and sliced
2 kiwi fruit, peeled and sliced
100 g/4 oz black cherries
3–4 tablespoons Cointreau
10 vegetarian macaroons or other
   crumbly biscuits

For the topping:
200 ml/7 fl oz Greek yogurt

200 ml/7 fl oz crème fraîche
100 g/4 oz light brown soft sugar

For the vegan* topping:
175 g/6 oz ground almonds
150 ml/¼ pint water
maple syrup, to taste
150 ml/¼ pint soya cream

To decorate:
8 strawberries, halved and fanned
few sprigs of mint

TIP
■

If you have tall sundae glasses, layer the fruit, biscuits and topping in each glass and chill. Just before serving, gently melt the sugar with 2–3 tablespoons of water in a saucepan and bring to the boil, stirring continuously. Boil until caramelized, then drizzle a little over each serving.

■ Place the prepared fruit in the base of a 900-ml/1½-pint ovenproof dish and drizzle with Cointreau. Crumble the macaroons or other biscuits over the top of the fruit.

■ Mix the yogurt and crème fraîche together and spoon over to seal in the fruit completely. Chill in the refrigerator for at least 1 hour. If making the vegan topping, place all the ingredients in a blender and blend until smooth. Spoon over the fruit as before.

■ Sprinkle the sugar over the topping and place under a preheated hot grill for 2–3 minutes, until the sugar melts and bubbles.

■ Serve decorated with fanned strawberry halves and mint sprigs.

Serves 4–6

APRICOT CHOCOLATE
REFRIGERATOR CAKE

TIP

■

Look for plain chocolate with a high cocoa butter content for quality and make sure that it is completely dairy-free. If you are making this dessert vegan, some of the supermarket own-brand deluxe cooking chocolates are suitable.

This is a grown-up variation of 'Tiffin', the 'no cook' chocolate, fruit and biscuit cake. The Amaretto liqueur makes it really special. At Christmas you can buy apricots bottled in Amaretto, but it is easy enough to marinate dried apricots in the liqueur for a few hours before making the cake.

100 g/4 oz good quality plain vegan chocolate
100 g/4 oz butter or vegan margarine*
2 tablespoons golden syrup
1 tablespoon milk or soya milk*
250 g/9 oz vegan digestive or almond biscuits, crushed
100 g/4 oz apricots in Amaretto liqueur
50 g/2 oz chopped roast hazelnuts or almonds
sliced apricots, to decorate
150 ml/5 fl oz double cream, whipped (omit for vegans*)

Apricot coulis:
100 g/4 oz canned apricots, drained
1 teaspoon Amaretto liqueur

■ Melt the chocolate in a bowl over a saucepan of hot water.
■ In a separate bowl, also over a saucepan of simmering water, melt the butter or vegan margarine*, golden syrup and milk together.
■ Stir the melted chocolate and crushed biscuits into the golden syrup mixture and mix well. Add the apricots and nuts, and mix well.
■ Grease and line a 450-g/1-lb loaf tin with baking parchment. Spoon in the chocolate biscuit mixture, press down well and chill for 2 hours.
■ Make the coulis: purée the apricots and Amaretto in a blender or press through a sieve.
■ Serve the cake sliced with some apricot coulis, sliced apricots and whipped cream (optional).

Serves 6–8

Opposite: Apricot chocolate refrigerator cake

INDIVIDUAL APPLE
CHARLOTTES

TIP

∎

If the apples are a little too sharp for your taste, stir a little sugar into the warm purée.

Nobody would guess that these little puddings are dairy- and egg-free. They make a light but filling winter dessert, the apple purée in the centre being an unexpected surprise.

225 g/8 oz Bramley apples, peeled, cored and sliced
2 tablespoons vegan sweet cider
grated zest and juice of 1 lemon
½ teaspoon ground cinnamon
75 g/3 oz soft vegan margarine
4 tablespoons maple syrup or soft brown sugar
1 tablespoon soya flour mixed with 2 tablespoons water

75 g/3 oz ground almonds
25 g/1 oz soya flour
½ teaspoon baking powder
½ teaspoon almond essence

To serve:
icing sugar, for dusting
4 strawberries
few sprigs of mint
soya cream

∎ Preheat the oven to 180°C/350°F/Gas Mark 4.
∎ Cook the apple slices in the cider and lemon juice. Add the lemon zest and cinnamon and purée well.
∎ Cream the margarine with the maple syrup or sugar. Mix the soya flour and water together and stir into the creamed mixture.
∎ Stir in the ground almonds, soya flour, baking powder and almond essence.
∎ Grease 4 individual ramekins and divide two-thirds of the sponge mixture equally between them. Use a teaspoon to make an indentation in the centre and ease the mixture up the sides.
∎ Put the apple purée into the centre of each sponge, leaving enough room to top each one with the remaining sponge mixture.
∎ Place on a baking sheet and bake in the preheated oven for 15–20 minutes, until firm and golden.
∎ Dust with icing sugar and decorate with strawberries and mint sprigs. Serve hot with soya cream.

Serves 4

MINCEMEAT AND
APRICOT CRUMBLE TART

*CAN BE VEGAN

Vegetarian mincemeat is widely available in both basic and luxury versions. You can use a basic mincemeat in this recipe and transform it into a luxury one by the addition of the brandied apricots. This festive tart is equally delicious served hot or cold.

225 g/8 oz dried apricots

8 tablespoons brandy

225 g/8 oz ready-made shortcrust pastry

450-g/1-lb jar vegetarian mincemeat

225 g/8 oz Bramley apples, peeled and cored

juice of 1 lemon

toasted flaked almonds, to decorate

cream, crème fraîche, or soya cream*, to serve

Crumble topping:

50 g/2 oz plain flour

50 g/2 oz ground almonds

50 g/2 oz butter or vegan margarine*

50 g/2 oz soft brown sugar

TIP

■

Ready-made shortcrust pastry can be bought in most supermarkets. It is a great time saver in a busy festive season but, of course, you can make your own if you prefer.

■ Preheat the oven to 200°C/400°F/Gas Mark 6. Marinate the dried apricots in the brandy for at least 1 hour.

■ Roll out the pastry and use to line a 22-cm/9-in loose-bottomed flan ring. Prick the base with a fork and rest in the refrigerator for 30 minutes. Line with baking parchment and baking beans and bake 'blind' for about 10–15 minutes in the preheated oven. Remove from the oven and allow to cool a little.

■ Chop up the marinated apricots and stir into the mincemeat with any remaining brandy. Use to fill the base of the pastry case.

■ Slice the prepared apples, dip in lemon juice to prevent them discolouring and arrange on top of the mincemeat.

■ For the crumble topping: mix the flour and ground almonds in a bowl, rub in the butter or vegan margarine* and stir in the sugar.

■ Sprinkle the crumble topping on top of the apples and bake for 30–40 minutes, until golden.

■ Decorate with toasted almonds and serve with cream, crème fraîche or vegan soya cream*.

Serves 6

*CAN BE VEGAN

PEAR, BRANDY AND
HAZELNUT STRUDEL

Most strudel recipes use filo pastry. This one is different in that it uses very thinly rolled puff pastry which gives a richer and flakier result than filo and is easier to eat!

450 g / 1 lb dessert pears (Comice, Conference, Rocha or William)
50 g / 2 oz chopped roasted hazelnuts
25 g / 1 oz brown sugar
50 g / 2 oz sultanas
½ teaspoon ground cinnamon
1 tablespoon brandy
225 g / 8 oz ready-made puff pastry
25 g / 1 oz butter or vegan margarine*
icing sugar, for dusting

■ Preheat the oven to 200°C/400°F/Gas Mark 6.
■ Peel, core and chop the pears and mix in a bowl with the hazelnuts, sugar, sultanas, cinnamon and brandy.
■ Roll out the puff pastry very thinly — you should be able to see the pattern of the work top through it.
■ Melt the butter or vegan margarine* in a small saucepan and brush over the surface of the pastry. Place the filling at one narrow end and roll up, folding in the sides to enclose the filling as you go.
■ Place on a greased baking sheet, brush with more butter or margarine* and make a couple of cuts in the top.
■ Bake in the preheated oven for about 20 minutes, until the pastry is well risen and golden. Dust the strudel with icing sugar and serve hot with custard, cream or soya cream*.

Serves 4

TIP
■

An alternative way of using the hazelnuts in this recipe is to leave them out of the mixture and sprinkle them over the whole surface of the pastry which has been brushed with fat instead. When the strudel is rolled up, you get crunchy hazelnuts between each flaky layer of the pastry.

STICKY GINGER AND
LEMON SYRUP CAKE

This is a wonderfully sticky cake, partly because of the lemon syrup which is poured over and allowed to soak into the warm cake as it comes out of the oven. A spoonful of crème fraîche complements the flavour and freshens the palette.

225 g/8 oz self-raising flour
½ teaspoon bicarbonate of soda
2 teaspoons ground ginger
100 g/4 oz butter
4 tablespoons molasses
125 g/5 oz muscovado sugar
grated zest and juice of 1 lemon
1 free-range egg, beaten

2 tablespoons milk
2 pieces stem ginger in syrup,
   chopped

To serve:
quartered slices of lemon
crème fraîche

> **TIP**
> ■
> Stir a little of the ginger syrup into the crème fraîche before serving or use fromage frais as an alternative.

■ Preheat the oven to 180°C/350°F/Gas Mark 4.

■ In a bowl, sift the flour, bicarbonate of soda and ground ginger together.

■ Melt the butter in a saucepan with the molasses and 100 g/4 oz of the sugar. Cool slightly, then add the lemon zest and whisk in the egg and milk. Pour the liquid ingredients into the flour, then add the chopped ginger in syrup and beat well.

■ Turn into a greased and lined 900-g/2-lb loaf tin. Bake in the preheated oven for 40–45 minutes, until risen and firm to the touch.

■ Warm the lemon juice in a saucepan and stir in the remaining 25 g/1 oz sugar until dissolved. Pierce the top of the cake with a skewer and pour the syrup over the cake. Leave to cool, then turn out.

■ Decorate the cake with quartered slices of lemon. Cut into slices and serve with a spoonful of crème fraîche.

Serves 8

STRAWBERRY
LAYER GATEAU

This is a classic summer dessert. Now that English strawberries are available from June to September, you can make it right through the summer months. You will need two 18-cm/7-in sandwich tins, which have been greased and floured.

175 g/6 oz soft vegetarian margarine
175 g/6 oz caster sugar
175 g/6 oz white self-raising flour
3 free-range eggs, beaten
1/2 teaspoon vanilla essence
2 teaspoons hot water
600 ml/1 pint whipping cream
150 ml/5 fl oz Kirsch or other liqueur
450 g/1 lb fresh strawberries
100 g/4 oz flaked almonds, toasted

■ Preheat the oven to 190°C/375°F/Gas Mark 5.
■ Put the margarine, caster sugar, self-raising flour, eggs, vanilla essence and hot water into a mixing bowl and beat until smooth. Divide equally between the two prepared cake tins and bake in the preheated oven for about 20 minutes, until the sponge is golden and springs back to the touch.
■ Leave to cool in the tins for 5 minutes, then turn out onto a wire rack and allow to cool completely. Cut each sponge in half horizontally so that you have 4 layers.
■ Whip the cream until stiff and fold in the Kirsch. Put about a quarter of the cream to one side for the decoration.
■ Reserve 6 evenly sized strawberries and slice the rest. Spread each layer of sponge with some cream and top with the strawberries. Make sure you leave enough cream to coat the top and sides of the gâteau. Smooth the top.
■ Coat the sides of the gâteau with toasted almonds. Use the reserved cream to pipe rosettes on the top. Halve the reserved strawberries and use to decorate. Chill until required.

Serves 6–8

Opposite: Strawberry layer gâteau

LEMON
MILLE FEUILLES

L ight and refreshing, this fresh-tasting citrus dessert is an excellent dairy-free end to a meal.

225 g/8 oz ready-made puff pastry
a little soya milk, for brushing

300 ml/½ pint water
50 g/2 oz vegan margarine

Lemon filling:
4 tablespoons cornflour
50 g/2 oz caster sugar
zest of 2 large lemons
juice of 1 lemon

To garnish:
150 ml/¼ pint soya cream
icing sugar for dusting
4 strawberries, fanned
4 sprigs of fresh mint

■ Preheat the oven to 200°C/400°F/Gas Mark 6.
■ Roll out the pastry and cut into 4 pieces, 7 x 12 cm/3 x 5 in. Place on a greased baking sheet, brush with soya milk and cook in the preheated oven for 10–15 minutes. When risen and golden, remove from the oven and allow to cool on a wire rack, then separate each piece into 3 layers.
■ Mix the cornflour and sugar together in a bowl. Add enough water from the measured 300 ml/½ pint to mix to a smooth paste.
■ Put the rest of the water and the lemon zest in a saucepan, bring to the boil and then pour over the cornflour and sugar mixture, stirring until smooth.
■ Return to the saucepan and bring back to the boil, stirring all the time. Reduce the heat and simmer for 1 minute. Remove from the heat, and beat in the margarine and then the lemon juice. Allow to cool and thicken.
■ Beat the lemon mixture thoroughly until smooth and shiny. Keeping the layers of pastry in the right order, spread half the lemon mixture on the bottom slices, top with the middle slices and spread the remaining mixture over these. Top with the final pastry layers and place on serving plates.
■ Pour a little soya cream around the plate. Dust each mille feuille with icing sugar and decorate with a fanned strawberry and mint sprigs.

Serves 4

FLORENTINES

*CAN BE VEGAN

These contrast well with the pear and stem ginger sorbet on page 244. You can use any mixture of nuts and fruits that you fancy to change the flavour of these delicate biscuits. The chocolate coating is optional.

50 g/2 oz butter or vegan margarine*
50 g/2 oz caster sugar
25 g/1 oz blanched, chopped almonds
25 g/1 oz chopped roasted hazelnuts
50 g/2 oz vegetarian glacé cherries, chopped
25 g/1 oz mixed peel, finely chopped
2 teaspoons lemon juice
100 g/4 oz vegan plain chocolate*

■ Preheat the oven to 180°C/350°F/Gas Mark 4. Line 2 baking sheets with non-stick baking parchment.
■ Melt the butter or vegan margarine* in a saucepan. Add the sugar and boil the mixture for 1 minute, stirring all the time. Remove the pan from the heat and add all the remaining ingredients, except the chocolate, and stir well to mix.
■ Drop the mixture in very small heaps onto the prepared baking sheet, allowing each room to spread (9 on each sheet).
■ Bake in the preheated oven for 10–15 minutes, until golden brown (watch carefully as the edges tend to burn). Remove from the oven and use the edge of a knife to neaten the edges of the biscuits. Leave on the baking sheets to cool.
■ Melt the chocolate over a bowl of simmering water (or for 2–3 minutes in microwave). Take each biscuit off the baking parchment and spread chocolate thinly over the smooth (flat) side. Leave to start setting and just before it sets use a fork to mark wavy lines in the chocolate. Leave to cool completely.

Makes 18

TIP

■

Make sure you leave these little biscuits to cool completely before you try to remove them from the baking parchment as they are quite fragile.

CHOCOLATE AND
CHESTNUT TORTE

This is a very rich dessert, especially for chocoholics! You only need a small slice but will probably be tempted to have more!

TIP
■
You can buy sweetened chestnut purée in a can. As you only need 50 g/2 oz for this recipe, weigh the remainder into 50 g/2 oz portions, wrap in cling film, label and freeze.

50 g/2 oz plain chocolate
50 g/2 oz unsalted butter
2 free-range eggs, separated
50 g/2 oz sweetened chestnut
  purée
12 g/½ oz plain flour
good pinch of cream of tartar
1 tablespoon granulated sugar

Topping:
350 ml/12 fl oz double cream
4 tablespoons Tia Maria or other
  coffee liqueur
50 g/2 oz plain chocolate, grated
  very finely (use food processor disk)
chocolate coated coffee beans
  (optional)

■ Preheat the oven to 180°C/350°F/Gas Mark 4. Grease and then line a 20-cm/8-in loose-bottomed cake tin.

■ Break the chocolate into small pieces and place them with the butter in a bowl over a pan of gently simmering water. Stir until melted and smooth.

■ Put the egg yolks, chestnut purée and flour in a large bowl and whisk together. Stir in the melted chocolate and butter mixture.

■ Whisk the egg whites and cream of tartar together in a grease-free bowl until they form soft peaks. Then gradually sprinkle on the granulated sugar and whisk the mixture until stiff. Gently fold into the chocolate mixture, using a metal spoon.

■ Pour into the prepared cake tin and level the top. Cook in the preheated oven for 35–40 minutes. Allow to sit for 5 minutes, then remove the cake from the tin and leave to cool on a wire cooling rack.

■ To make the topping, whisk the double cream until stiff and gently fold in the Tia Maria.

■ Spread a layer of cream over the top of the torte and then, using a piping bag and star nozzle, pipe rosettes around the edge of the torte. Sprinkle the grated chocolate over the centre and, if liked, decorate the edge with chocolate coated coffee beans. Chill for at least 2 hours, or until required.

Serves 8–10

CHOCOLATE ESPRESSO
AND ROASTED PECAN TORTE

SUITABLE FOR VEGANS

This cake is extremely rich and luxurious, but completely dairy-free. It is ideal for any celebration. The addition of espresso gives the flavour an exciting twist. This quantity makes a very large torte. You may prefer to bake it in two tins and sandwich together with some of the fudge icing.

1.3 litres/2¼ pints boiling water
200 g/7 oz creamed coconut
2 tablespoons powdered espresso coffee
800 g/1 lb 12 oz self-raising flour
100 g/4 oz cocoa powder
2 teaspoons baking powder
100 g/4 oz roasted pecans
300 g/12 oz light muscovado sugar

420 ml/14 fl oz vegetable oil
2 tablespoons brandy

Fudge icing:
100 g/4 oz vegan margarine
2 teaspoons brandy
100 g/4 oz cocoa powder
6 tablespoons water
550 g/1 lb 4 oz icing sugar
few drops of vanilla essence

TIP
■
Serve with a mixture of colourful fresh fruit, such as strawberries, kiwi, melon and peaches, cut into chunks and threaded on skewers to make kebabs. Not only does this look exciting but the fruit helps to freshen the palette after the richness of the torte.

■ Preheat the oven to 180°C/350°F/Gas Mark 4. Grease and line a 27.5-cm/11-in cake tin.

■ Dissolve the espresso coffee in 2 tablespoons of the boiling water.

■ Place the creamed coconut in a large bowl and cover with the remaining boiling water. Stir until dissolved.

■ Mix together the flour, cocoa powder, baking powder, pecans and sugar.

■ Add the espresso coffee to the cake mixture with the oil. Stir thoroughly, then add the cooled, dissolved coconut mixture and incorporate well.

■ Pour the mixture into the prepared cake tin and bake in the preheated oven for approximately 1½ hours, or until the cake feels springy to the touch. Leave to cool slightly before turning out onto a cooling rack. When the cake is cool, drizzle with the brandy.

■ To make the fudge icing, put all the ingredients in a food processor and blend until smooth. Spread the icing evenly over the cake and then use a fork to make an attractive pattern across the top.

Serves 12–16

GLOSSARY OF INGREDIENTS

AGAR AGAR

Also known as kanten or china grass, this sea vegetable is used as a vegetarian alternative to gelatine. Usually found in flaked or, occasionally, powdered form from a health food shop. Flakes are probably the best to use as they are processed using natural rather than chemical methods.

ARAME

This sea vegetable is rich in calcium and iodine. If you are unfamiliar with the taste and texture of sea vegetables, this is a good one to start with as it has a mild flavour and is softer in texture than some of the others. Being black in colour, it provides an excellent contrast in salads and stir-fries. Soak it for at least 5 minutes in warm water, or 10 minutes in cold, before using.

BUCKWHEAT

A gluten-free grain that has a strong, earthy flavour. You can buy raw whole buckwheat, roasted buckwheat (also known as kasha), buckwheat flour (traditionally used for crêpes in Brittany and blinis in Russia) or soba (buckwheat) noodles. Buckwheat contains rutin which is good for poor circulation.

CAPERS

Usually pickled in brine or packed in salt, with or without their leaves, these are the flower buds of a bush that grows around the Mediterranean. Capers have a strong and distinctive flavour and should be used sparingly or they will overpower a dish.

CELERIAC

A knobbly root vegetable with a strong, sweet celery flavour. Prepare it as you would a swede or turnip by peeling off the outer 'skin' and cutting the flesh into chunks. It can be boiled, steamed or fried, or roasted after parboiling. It's delicious boiled, then mashed with potatoes.

CEPS

Also known as porcini ('little pigs' in Italian) because of their shape. These are wild mushrooms, usually purchased in dried form. They need reconstituting before use. Ceps have a very rich, intense flavour and the dried mushrooms can be ground to a fine powder and added to soups or stews to enrich the flavours.

FETA CHEESE

This is a Greek cheese which is traditionally made from sheeps' milk although most sold commercially nowadays is made from cows' milk. It has quite a sour salty flavour and crumbly texture, and although it is good in salads, it is also useful in cooking as it doesn't lose its shape.

FROMAGE FRAIS

A soft cream cheese that varies between one and eight per cent fat content. It is usually thickened with a culture, and vegetarians should check the label on the carton to make sure that animal rennet has not been used. It is non-acidic and goes well with fruit. It is also useful in cooking, especially in soups and sauces, as it does not curdle if boiled.

GARAM MASALA

An Indian spice mixture. Although this can be bought ready mixed, you will obtain a better flavour by mixing your own selection of (seven) spices when required. Experiment until you find the mix of ingredients in the proportions that you like best.

GRANOLA

This is toasted muesli and tends to be higher in fat and sugar than muesli.

HIZIKI

Also spelt hijiki, this is a sun-dried and coarsely shredded sea vegetable from Japan. Hiziki translates as the 'bearer of wealth and beauty'. It is similar in appearance to arame but has a more chewy texture. It is rich in calcium, iron and fibre and should be soaked before use.

LEMON GRASS

A very distinctive ingredient in Thai and other South-east Asian cuisines, this fragrant herb has become widely available in the West. There is no substitute for the fresh lemon grass; in dried and powdered form, it is a pale shadow of the fresh flavour. If you are unable to obtain fresh lemon grass, substitute lemon zest instead. It can be used in both sweet and savoury dishes.

MAPLE SYRUP

This sweetening agent is obtained from the sap of the maple trees in Canada and North America. The sap is heated and concentrated to give a rich colour and flavour. It takes between 35–50 gallons of sap to make one gallon of syrup. Beware of cheap maple-flavoured syrups which may contain only two per cent maple syrup. It can be used as a substitute for honey in many dishes, which makes it a useful ingredient for anyone on a strict vegan diet.

MILLET

A gluten-free grain consisting of tiny, yellow, hulled balls. Millet has a very light texture when cooked and is high in iron, protein and the B group of vitamins. It can be used in place of rice in salads, bakes and risottos and should be cooked for about 15 minutes in three times the amount of water to grain. You can also buy millet flakes and millet flour.

MIRIN

This is a Japanese sweet cooking wine. It is always used for cooking and is never drunk by the glass. Mirin is made by fermenting yeasted rice grains over a period of about six months. It is used in oriental cooking to balance salty seasonings and to enhance the flavours of vinegared dishes, such as dressings, dips, sauces and glazes. If you are unable to obtain it, then a vegetarian sherry is the nearest substitute.

MISO

This savoury paste is formed by combining cooked soya beans with grains, yeasted grains and sea salt, which are then left to ferment for one to two years. It is rich in protein, B vitamins and minerals. Use sparingly as it is strongly flavoured, and blend with a little water or stock before adding to a soup or stew to ensure that it is properly mixed into the dish. It should be stored in a covered container in a cool place although it should not be necessary to refrigerate it. Sometimes a white yeast activity will be seen on the surface of the miso. This is not harmful and can be stirred back in. The most commonly found miso in this country is barley or mugi miso. You may also find genmai (kome) or rice miso, hatcho (no grain) miso, or sweet white miso.

MOLASSES

A by-product of sugar refining. It contains 50–70 per cent sucrose, the remainder being water and the nutrients from the original cane, plus calcium and iron from the processing which can be significant if iron vats are used for storing the product. Unsulphured blackstrap molasses is the best to buy. In ordinary molasses, traces of the sulphur used in the processing may remain; and Barbados molasses, which is made from cane juice which has been filtered and boiled, lacks the nutrient content of blackstrap.

MOOLI

Also known as daikon or white radish, this is an oriental member of the radish family. It looks like a very large, white, smooth parsnip and can be sliced and cooked in stir fries, or grated and eaten raw in a salad. It contains a high level of vitamin C.

PASSATA

Cooked and sieved tomatoes. Passata can usually be bought in a bottle or tetra pack and adds a lovely rich flavour to soups, stews or sauces, wherever a strong tomato flavour is required.

PINE NUTS OR KERNELS

These nuts have become very popular and, although expensive, can be used sparingly because of their strong flavour. Often better toasted, they can be used in salads, stir-fries, quiches, and to make pesto. They have a high oil content and should be refrigerated or frozen as they quickly become rancid.

QUARK

A soft, low-fat curd cheese which is traditionally made in Germany. It is very useful in sauces and in pâtés.

QUINOA

Pronounced 'keen-wah', this gluten-free grain is very useful in a vegetarian diet as it is an excellent source of protein. This is the sacred grain of the Incas, but is now grown in the UK. Use it wherever you would use rice or bulgar wheat. Cook for about 15 minutes in three times the amount of water to grain.

SAMBAL OELEK

Indonesian chilli paste. This is very hot so use sparingly.

SHOYU

A light soy sauce made by fermenting soya beans with sea salt and water and ageing for at least 18 months. Shoyu contains wheat and is therefore not suitable for anyone suffering from a wheat or gluten allergy. It has a lighter flavour than tamari.

SOURED CREAM

About 18 per cent fat content (the same as single cream), so use sparingly. Cream is pasteurized and homogenized and is then soured by the addition of a lactic acid starter culture. You can sour single cream with the addition of a little lemon juice, if preferred.

SOYA CREAM

A very useful non-dairy cream made from soya beans. It is similar in consistency to single cream and can be used as a substitute for cream, either stirred into dishes to give a creamy flavour and texture, or poured over desserts.

SPELT FLOUR

This grain is similar to wheat and originated in the Middle East. It was reintroduced to Britain fairly recently and is now grown on a commercial scale. It is extremely good for bread-making, being high in protein. It also appears to cause less problems for some sufferers of grain allergies. It is highly water-soluble and easy to digest. You can also buy spelt pasta.

SZECHUAN PEPPER

Also known as Sichuan pepper, fagara and anise pepper, this spice is not related to the black and white peppercorns with which we are familiar in Western cookery. Szechuan pepper is the red-brown berry of a Chinese ash tree. It is one of the constituents of Chinese five-spice powder.

TAHINI

Sesame seeds creamed with oil. Although it has a high fat content, the sesame seeds are a good source of calcium and zinc which cannot be accessed unless the seeds are crushed or creamed. Most commonly found in hummus, it also makes a delicious breakfast spread when mixed with a little yeast extract, and can be used to thicken soups and stews or to bind savoury loaves (e.g. nut loaf) in place of egg.

TAMARI

A dark soy sauce made by fermenting soya beans with sea salt and water and ageing for at least 18 months. Unlike shoyu, tamari is wheat-free and has a rich, deep flavour which is useful in soups, stews and stir-fries.

TERIYAKI

This is a tamari based marinating sauce with added ingredients, such as sweet rice wine, rice vinegar, plum juice and garlic. However, it is not usually suitable for anyone following a strict vegan diet as it usually contains honey.

TOFU

Tofu or bean curd is made from the humble soya bean. The beans are processed to make soya 'milk' which is then curdled, in a process similar to cheese-making, to produce tofu. It can be bought in firm blocks, which may be plain, smoked or marinated, and are good for savoury dishes, such as stir-fries, pâtés and stews, or in a softer form – 'silken' tofu – which is best used for desserts or as an egg and cream substitute in flans where a smoother, runnier texture is required. It is very high in protein, very low in saturated fats, low in carbohydrates, cholesterol-free and rich in calcium, vitamins and minerals.

WASABI

Also known as Japanese horseradish, this can be found in powdered or paste form in Chinese and Japanese supermarkets. It is even stronger than ordinary horseradish and should be added to dishes with care. It is usually used as a condiment with sushi and is bright green in colour.

INDEX

Numbers in italics refer to photographs.

THE VEGETARIAN SOCIETY

The Vegetarian Society is the official voice of vegetarianism in the United Kingdom. The Society exists to promote Vegetarianism in the UK and throughout the world through research, national campaigns, education, liaison with the food industry and via our cookery school.

A registered charity established in 1847, the Society is the leading authority on vegetarian issues, providing expert information on the vegetarian diet, for the benefit of animal welfare, human health and the environment. The Society provides information and resources for use by the public, media, health professionals, schools and opinion formers.

Members of the Society receive a full-colour quarterly magazine full of the latest news, features and recipes, a discount card for use at hundreds of establishments, a unique seedling logo badge, access to our membership hotline and reduced rate subscription to *Wildlife* magazine. Membership support is vital to the Society's promotional and campaigning work. Members can become actively involved in the Society's work through the local group network or through the Council of Trustees, elected from the members.

The Society runs its own cookery school, Cordon Vert, the home of excellent vegetarian cuisine. The School runs inspirational courses to suit all abilities and interests from day courses through to a four-week Diploma course. Whatever your interest – Italian, Middle Eastern, Indian, Cajun or Thai cuisine – the Cordon Vert Cookery School has something to offer.

The Society works with major food manufacturers and retailers to improve the quality, quantity and variety of vegetarian food available, The Society also runs its own licence scheme, known as the seedling symbol, approving over 2,000 products which are guaranteed to be 100 per cent vegetarian.

The Vegetarian Society needs membership support if it is to continue to operate at all levels to spread the vegetarian message. For a free vegetarian starter pack or details of the Cordon Vert Cookery School, please call us on 0161 925 2000 or write to the address below:

The Vegetarian Society
Parkdale
Dunham Road
Altrincham
Cheshire WA14 4QG

E-Mail address is HYPERLINK mailto:info@vegsoc.org

Internet address: HYPERLINK http://www.vegsoc.org